PRECYCLE!

D0067574

by

Paul Peacock

Published by The Good Life Press Ltd. 2008

ISBN 978 1 90487 138 5
A catalogue record for this book is available from
the British Library.

Published by
The Good Life Press Ltd.
PO Box 536
Preston
PR2 9ZY

www.goodlifepress.co.uk
www.homefarmer.co.uk

Set by The Good Life Press Ltd.

Printed and bound in Great Britain
by Cromwell Press

PRECYCLE!

by Paul Peacock

CONTENTS

CONTENTS

Precycle!

Foreword

Would it surprise you that you could make a carpet cleaner for pennies that costs pounds? That you can make your own bacon and good bacon at that – far better than you can buy, for almost the price of cheap pork? Would you like to be able to make sauces at a penny a bottle or bread for a third of the price? Would it surprise you that the majority of the powder in automatic washing powder is simply washing soda and that this product works better for a fraction of the cost?

Amongst all the fear and financial turmoil the world is experiencing, this book points a finger towards a different way of living and shows that much of what is packaged for our convenience is all too frequently too expensive, too polluting and often ineffectual.

It was borne out of an idea that the food I buy from the supermarket often has ingredients that are not for me at all, but rather for the seller of the product in order to make it last longer on a shelf. Well, we decided simply to leave it on the shelf and make our own. Perhaps you will join us?

Precycle!

Yes, of course you have to buy the ingredients from the shops, but the idea of the book is to take us all one step closer to the things we buy, the food we eat, the cleaning materials we use in the house and the beauty products we put on our skin.

In short, this is a trip around the supermarket and points out how you can make what you find on the shelves. This book is incomplete in as much as the whole of what we buy changes every day. The fundamental idea is to show people it is possible to make what we consume ourselves rather than buy it from the shops. Precycle! demonstrates a way of living that makes rather than consumes.

I would like to thank Diana Sutton for many of the recipes contained in this book and Ruth Tott and Paul Melnyczuk for having the foresight of publishing it.

One final point. When the book has become too old and tired, soak it in water and seed it with mushrooms. Grow yourself some brilliant fungi and make an omelette!

Paul Peacock
Manchester, England.
September 2008.

Introduction

When I was a boy we used to have two dustbins. One was for rubbish and the other was for food. Whatever food scraps we had went into the swill bin which was collected once a week by the pig man. Everyone had a swill bin. The scraps were collected and fed to the pigs, and in return for this we all got a turkey at Christmas. The other bin was for household rubbish and was collected once a week by the council. The dustbin men, many whom were semi-professional rugby league players, came to the back of the house and lifted the bins onto their backs, carrying them to the cart.

The bin was never full. This was partly because anything that would burn went into the fire. Milk bottles went back to the milkman. Beer and lemonade bottles went back to the shop, especially because there was 'thrupence' (3d, around 1.5p, which was enough to buy a telephone call, so about 40p today) deposit. As children we used to go around the neighbourhood asking for bottles and when we had collected about four or five

Precycle!

we could get ourselves some sweets.

There was no such thing as plastic. Anything wrapped in plastic was considered to be cheap and since people did not shop in supermarkets there were very few boxes. Boxes and excess packaging are now the norm to limit the damage of goods over land and sea and to make them sit on the shelf in an enticing 'come buy me' sort of way. Years ago we used to get our food wrapped in paper. Even eggs came loose in those days.

Today we have three waste bins. They are not all collected in the same week. They alternate. There are also some plastic bags for waste paper. There is a bin for plastic and metals, one for garden waste and one for everything else. We recycle most of the things we throw away and some of it is probably made into waste bins.

But fundamentally the way we shop and buy our provisions, and everything else for that matter, is wasteful. Recycled or not, we now have three full bins when once we couldn't even fill one, and to be honest I haven't yet mentioned the days when I have to drive to the local waste disposal centre (it used to be called the tip) with the odd bag of rubbish that won't fit in the bin.

The point of Precycle! is to make recycling redundant. Taken by itself, that statement is anathema. I am not advocating that we simply throw all the rubbish away. I abhor waste like everyone else. It is ingrained into our daily lives, mostly because this is how things are sold, but it doesn't have to be like that. Where once your meat was wrapped in paper, it is now parcelled in a little plastic box that frankly you can do nothing with. So why not shop at the butchers? You can't! Over 90% of butchers have gone out of business. Many people simply have no option other than to shop at the supermarket.

So, what is the point of Precycle!? Well, it's about making your own. Take wine, for example. So often these days people buy wine in boxes. The thought is that you are saving money by buying a lot of wine and somehow it is greener because you save on six bottles. But you do have a box to dispose of and a plastic liner and a tap.

You can, if you are a little patient, make 30 litres of fantastic wine (believe me, fantastic wine!) for the price of your 3 litre wine box and have almost zero impact on the environment with no waste to throw away and, if you bottle the wine, which isn't always necessary, you have used something that otherwise would take a lot of energy to recycle.

Recycling is costly in energy terms. The waste is transported somewhere using petrol. It is washed and sorted and, taking glass for an example, is heated to over 1100°C to melt it. When you wash out the bottles at home and sterilise them for bottling wine, you are actually contributing to saving the planet.

Precycling is about making the products instead of buying them. Growing your own tomatoes to make not just ketchup but brilliant ketchup a million times better and cheaper than you would buy in the shops, or buying loose tomatoes to do the same.

Precycling is making the things you need rather than allowing the manufacturers and supermarkets to dictate what you buy. It is doing away with the need to recycle by making it yourself; keeping the bottle and using it again and again.

Precycling is not to do with finances. In fact it has nothing to do with money at all. The Americans have a term 'monetizing' which is applied to websites. You make your website in such a way that you can earn cash. They do the same with everything in life; the food we eat, the water that lands on our heads, our need to communicate and travel. Some supermarkets now sell car insurance to cover the cars we need to go to their shops to buy their stuff!

The problem with this point of view is that everything takes on a value: the value of money. This devalues the things that people do and make. Yes, you can buy jam from Poland for very little money, but this doesn't mean it isn't worth making your own. Of course you are going to take an hour making jam and this would represent a payment much less than the minimum wage. Isn't it better to work in an office, earn a lot of money and buy your jam from the supermarket?

No, No, No! It is only better if you value money more than the craft of your own hands and mind. See how money devalues! Diana, my wife, makes jam. It is the best jam in the world because she made it and no amount of money can buy it. I suppose that she could go out to work and earn the money to buy jam, but then she would not be making jam herself and all of our lives would suffer as a result. Life is all about values and when they say I am only worth such and such, I automatically say no. I am worth what I do, what I make, who I am. My life is filled with better values than money.

If you spend half an hour making bread every morning you enrich that 30 minutes by what you are doing and everyone else, including yourself, by what you are eating. And no matter what they say on the television, bread made by machine cannot be as good. I won't waste paper by going into the argument that you can be sure of what is going into your food, how good it is and how it tastes better and is safer for the environment. That all should be a given.

So go on! Make your bread and jam. You won't find an

accountant able to agree with the money side of what you do. But boy, he'll enjoy eating your food, drinking your beer, sitting on your furniture and eating your produce.

Everything you buy from a supermarket is perfect, identically perfect. Things you make yourself don't always work out like that. And so we try, and when disaster strikes we are tempted away to the perfect product somewhere on a shelf with its barcode praying to be scanned.

One aspect of this book is about learning. Picking up skills you thought you never had and making objects and products better than the perfection sold by the shops, though the shopkeeper might disagree with you. I'd defy anyone to make a chair out of wood from scratch for the first time and not end up with something that looks like a clothes horse. But I bet you could make your shelves, then your drawers and then move on slowly and simply so that, having honed your skills, you end up making your own fitted kitchen out of cleaned up pallets.

It takes a great deal of energy to recycle our rubbish, though not as much as it would to make items from the raw materials. In the UK alone the energy saved in recycling paper will in turn provide the energy for four million homes for a year. As you can imagine, the situation is much the same for glass and metal objects. There are huge benefits to do with recycling materials, but the energy requirements are still immense. The recycled paper industry alone uses enough energy to power ten million homes and that is not taking into consideration all the rushing about from home to recycling centres in trucks and cars.
This means, taking an average figure from all sorts of sources, that a tonne of recycled paper takes 10,000 kWh. of energy. So an average sheet of A4 recycled pa-

Precycle!

per will use as much energy as a one bar electric fire does in 3 minutes or enough to fry an egg. The only source of energy this planet has is the sun and this single sheet of A4 needs the equivalent of three square metres of land surface for an hour on a hot day. Imagine the investment in energy terms of all the things we recycle and then multiply this by some unknown factor when it comes to the use of raw materials!

Let us not even dwell on cars, televisions, computers, microwaves, mobile telephones, carpets, fridges, packaging and all the millions of things we use in life that are manufactured. No wonder we need several planet's worth of resources just to maintain our current way of life.

Even though we are surrounded by messages of restraint, we still consume resources at an amazing rate. This is because we all expect a better lifestyle and there are so many more of us on the planet who want to enjoy the comfort brought about by a monetary economy. But the problem is that we cannot keep on consuming resources, as everyone keeps on telling us. Scarily though, the message is just not getting through, but perhaps it is just not the right one in the first place.

The fundamental basis of recycling is to use the resources we throw away in order to make products we buy. This means a continued demand for manufactured products, a need to use the recycled waste products to justify their recycling and an economy that can respond to these needs by buying them. In order to maintain such an economy, considerable resources and energy are needed. The buzzword is sustainable development.

But even if 100% of our resources are recycled, without a change in lifestyle we will continue to squander away our resources. There is no such thing as sustainable development. You cannot continue to consume more and at the same time make it somehow last forever. The only real development that lasts is reduction, consuming less, not more, and reducing our impact, not maintaining it.

Take the humble tin of baked beans as an example. Currently a tin of baked beans costs next to nothing. It has been used as a price barometer for many years and a price war between respective baked bean manufacturers and supermarkets has brought the price of a tin of beans to less than half a cigarette. The financial value of beans is almost nil, but there is another cost. The agricultural cost of growing the beans, the impact of monoculture, conventional fertilisers, weed killers and insecticides, transportation, processing and cooking, the growing of tomatoes and all the same processes to produce and transport them. Then the making of steel, recycled or not, the production of tins, the labels, the filling and transport of beans; all of these have a cost. This cost is not financial but environmental. Everything we buy has two costs, a financial cost that we pay and an environmental cost, an earth cost if you like, that the planet pays. A tin of beans costs next to nothing in money terms but there is a considerable cost to the planet.

But in my larder there are a dozen large kilner jars, each full of baked beans in tomato sauce. In the world of cheap tins of beans they are expensive. It took hours of effort to prepare the ground, to sow and care for the plants and then to harvest the beans. To cook and prepare them took effort, heat and care and, more than anything else, time. I could have earned enough money to buy a thousand tins of beans in the time it took to make them, but all I have are twelve. Beans made like this are expensive when accounted for in terms of money and time.

Industrialists will tell you that the reason for factories

Precycle!

the size of a village, whatever they may produce, is the economy of scale. It is cheaper per tin to make a million tins of beans than to make just a dozen. And there is something in what they say if the economy is money. Of course it is cheaper in financial terms, but the earth costs of economies of scale are devastating. The planet does not give a discount on a million tonnes of baked beans. The price must be paid in full. The easy removal of a tin of beans from a supermarket shelf belies a whole series of planet-sized problems.

Another way of putting all this is to ask a simple question. What currency do you use? Now the planet doesn't use money at all, but this doesn't mean that things don't have a cost. For example, a swallow incurs a great cost when it flies from Africa to Europe; it is just not valued in monetary terms. A gun might have a financial cost, but anyone can see that it can also have a cost in terms of lives taken.

It comes down to what you actually value. Make that your currency! Now I am not advocating an economy based things other than money, nor am I advocating bartering, although there is nothing wrong with that. But when you come to make value judgements about the things that someone else has already made, a financial judgement (i.e. the cost), maybe you can evaluate it using different criteria.

Let us look at buying a fridge. If your fridge was made before the year 2000 then the chances are that it will be three times less efficient than a modern fridge. So anyone can see the logic in changing it. You might be tempted by the financial savings you will make over time. The running costs are going to be a third of what they were. Clearly finances are a good way of judging the viability of the transaction and the disposal will have an even greater impact.

But think again. What are you going to do with that money? An old fridge might cost £1.50 a week to run, whereas a new one might only cost 50p. But are you really going to use that £1 in a green way? Chances are that you will spend it without thinking on something that might be very un-green.

But if you weigh up your proposed transaction with a different currency, say the total amount of energy needed to both make and run the new fridge, then you might get a bit of a shock. Usually the energy needed to create something in the modern world far outweighs the energy it uses during its life. Your new purchase will cost more than you think. Working out the energy status of an object is not all that easy, but it should also include transport in addition to the manufacturing process.

Yet another way of looking at the purchase is the complexity of the materials in the build. Your new fridge contains chemicals that are new to the planet. There are something like 1500 new chemicals created every year and you might not wish to play a part in making more.

Similarly, you might have a currency that is designed around the fact that to replace your fridge the planet has to deal with the destruction of your old one.

In short, your currency should be based on what you value, not what someone else asks you to pay. I realise that people are still going to want money for your purchases, but this doesn't have to be a part of your own thinking.

In the UK a think tank was working on the problem of regeneration. It looked at the fact that northern towns and cities had received billions of pounds to regenerate them, but there had been no substantial returns for this financial outlay. It concluded that if people in the north wanted to achieve anything like the average wealth for the UK, they should up sticks and move to London and that a million jobs and homes should be created in the capital to accommodate them. They concluded that cities such as Liverpool might have been excellent places for business in Victorian times, but not these days.

This is true when the only arbiter of wealth is financial. At its most basic, the increase in resources that a human can get each year is his share of the sun's energy that falls on the planet and its various effects; the wind, rain, tides and so on (yes, I know the tides come from the moon!). If you use this as a measure of wealth then you suddenly get a completely different notion of who is rich. Imagine yourself living in a penthouse flat with a Rolls Royce in the garage and a private jet on the tarmac. You will have a fat bank balance and can make money. But if you think about it biologically, even the poorest peasant with a little land is richer. At least he can go on making a life for himself consistently over the generations. All your financial wealth can disappear overnight and you cannot grow a lot of food in a penthouse flat. Look at the present state of our own financial institutions and the high earners they employed!

We need to think of wealth as quality of life, not just how much you have in the bank or how much credit you have. This way we begin to tune in to different aspects of purchasing. Take soap making as an example. We buy huge quantities of soap and throw huge quantities of perfectly good fat into landfills. Soap is basically treated fat! So you go to the shop in a car, buy soap that has been driven about the country created with huge amounts of energy, packaging and indeed all the various business and presentational trappings that come with a bar of soap. Yet you pay only pennies for the soap. If you make your own it might cost a few more pennies, but imagine all the savings the planet gets when you cut out a whole industry to make your own. There might be cost implications in the financial world, but there are savings everwhere else.

How does this make you more wealthy? Pride, knowl-edge, independence and the knowledge that your soap was made by you, is perfect for your skin, your family, your situation and you can still make soap even when the soap factories might have rusted away! How wealthy do you need to be?

Sadly precycling isn't the complete answer, but it's a start. My beans, and there isn't that much of them, took hours to produce from seed to final product. But baked beans made in this way are 'no impact baked beans.' They can grow in the garden without pesticides and oil based agriculture. They can be cooked on a stove fuelled by home-grown wood. They can be cooked in tomatoes grown in the same way and put into glass jars that will be used again and again.

And this goes for everything in this book. Precycling is about breaking the cycle of consumer led recycling. But alas, there are hardly enough hours in the day to do it all and at the same time earn a financial living. And it is then that you realise how poor you really are. The need to earn a living, to pay the bills, cuts across one's ability to make stuff for yourself.

In this book there are recipes for cleaners, bleaches, dis-infectants, soaps and insecticides. There are some very important golden rules that you must follow. A young man poisoned himself by accident when the cleaning solution he was using to degrease a car turned into phosgene gas by the action of the light from his welding arc. He didn't know that the light and heat from the arc would convert the chlorinated degreasing chemical to a First World War poisonous gas. This illustrates a serious

Precycle!

point: DO NOT MIX CHEMICALS! Do not try to make your own insecticides from a cocktail of chemicals because this is illegal. You simply do not know what you are making.

The only insecticides we have in this book are single substance remedies that have been used for a long time without problems. The temptation to combine washing up liquid and a concoction of nettle juice and marigold juice to kill greenfly might be strong, but the chemistry of what you are producing is not only unknown, it is also potentially dangerous. The pharmaceutical and chemical industries have to prove that the products they sell are not only fit for purpose but are also completely safe and there is no way that you can do that in the garden shed.

Another problem is where the form or structure of something is changed to do something it was never designed for. One incidence of this is the collection of hot air from a flue. It would seem on the face of it that the exhaust from the boiler is going to waste so why not build a greenhouse around it and use all that energy. After all, we have paid for it. But the flue was designed to vent excess gasses out of the house and should never be used as an extra heating device. Any change in its efficiency could have disastrous effects in the house. Your boiler could start pumping out poisonous carbon monoxide!

Do not try to change the basic use of something unless you are completely sure it is safe to do so. Coloured glass bottles are very pretty on a shelf but do not make a load bearing wall – and I have seen both!

The same goes for chemicals. If you are thinking of making up a solution of something, work from basic principles and don't just expect a household chemical to be just at the right concentration for your needs. A lady was admitted to hospital because she decided to use oven cleaner instead of cream cleaner for worktops and it took all the skin off her arms. She was there for a very long time.

Rest assured that this book will only give you recipes for things that are totally safe.

For most of us there is a knowledge and skills gap between our position and that of our grandparents. As an example take liquid paraffin as a treatment for constipation. Hands up how many of you, if asked to prepare such a dreadful concoction, would go to the ironmongers (hardware shop) to buy the paraffin that we burn in the greenhouse heater? How many would have no clue where to get the paraffin at all? How many would go and ask the chemist for a bottle of the oily clear liquid? The point is that unfortunately we have had much of our knowledge 'shopped out.' We tend to use only those things readily available from the supermarket.

So, wherever necessary, this book will give big hints about where to get the ingredients and equipment you will need.

What Our Grandparents Did

Domestic life was different for our forebears. A hundred years ago people worked long hours and had the most tiresome of daily tasks both in and out of the home. Nobody wants to go back to a lifestyle so full of toil, servitude, inequality and injustice. But we are also led to believe that an enjoyable life is hardly possible without the trappings of the modern world. So I would like to compare the town where I now live with that of 60 years ago just to show that great culture isn't inextricably linked to today's modus operandi.

Precycle!

The population has remained pretty much the same at 40,000. There used to be two cinemas, now there are none. There were 40 butchers, now there is 1. There was a mechanics institute and a Worker's Education Institute; a couple of choirs, five brass bands, two dance halls, three football teams, a rugby league team and a cricket team. Of these, all that remains is the cricket team.

There was a tram system and a railway and the most beautiful civic gardens in the whole county. I say these things simply to point out that leisure time and a so called easy life do not necessarilry add up to a better quality of life. It seems that these days people have more time to do less.

Tools and Equipment

It is important that you get the very best quality tools and equipment, and by that I include kitchen utensils, pots and pans, knives and so on. We have almost forgotten how to recognise good tools these days because we are not expected to actually use them. But you can't expect to have to buy a new saucepan every couple of months, or a new saw. Precycling is about making your own and in order to do this you need good equipment. I bought a saw some years ago that simply couldn't cut in a straight line. It took me months of dejection thinking I was no good until I really watched what was going on. The blade was twisted; not much but just enough to make it cut in an arc. The saw is now being used to cut trees and things. It might even end its life as a musical instrument. You cannot afford poor, cheap tools; they really are are too expensive by any system of values!

Bottle it!

All Kinds of Sauces, Pickles. Jams and Preserves

Some people think that the only way to get their hands on sauce is to buy it from the shop. But someone had to make it for the first time. HP brown sauce, for example, used to be called Parliament Sauce and this is why there has always been a picture of the Houses of Parliament on the front, even in the plastic bottles, which seems a little odd, I think.

Before bottling anything you must make sure that your jars, bottles and other containers are sterile. To sterilise, take off any rubber seals if using kilner-type jars and the lids of screw top jars. Place the jars on a baking sheet and put in a preheated oven at 120°C (240°F, Gas mark ½) for ten minutes. Put the lids and/or rubber seals in boiling water and leave until required. Alternatively, place the jars in a Milton solution and follow the instructions on the pack as you would for baby feeding equipment. You could also use plain jars and dustcover-type discs of cloth as lids, securing them with rubber bands. These make pretty gifts and you can co-ordinate them

Precycle!

with kitchen furnishings. But for the best quality storage a sealed lid is desirable.

Finally, prior to the first recipes, I should also like to make a point regarding the measurements throughout the book. To provide 100% accurate conversions would require immensely detailed calculations with figures often running to 4 or 5 decimal places. You shouldn't need a mathematics degree to precycle! Recipes are also always best viewed as guidelines and measurements should be prone to change to accomodate individual tastes. Please view them as such and experiment with them to perfect your own versions of everything from peppermint tea to tomato ketchup.

Tomato Ketchup

Ketchup is a simple condiment to make and you can make it in huge or small quantities. This will make about 1.5 to 2 litres (nearly 5 pints) depending how thick you like it. The best tomatoes are Italian plum, but any will do. They don't even have to be uniformly ripe. Of course ketchup is rich in lycopene, which is a chemical related closely to masculine health and has anti-cancer properties.

You Will Need:

5kg (11lbs) tomatoes
2 large finely chopped onions
4 level tsps salt
5 minced garlic cloves
½ tsp black pepper
½ tsp cayenne pepper
220g (8oz) sugar
400ml (1 pint) cider vinegar

Plus a bouquet garni of a finger sized cinnamon stick, 5 whole cloves and 2 bay leaves. To make a bouquet garni get a square of muslin cloth, put the spices and herbs in the centre,tie with string so that it drops into the pan. Tie the other end of string round the handle base so you can remove it easily.

Peel your tomatoes by piecing them and placing them in a bowl of boiled water. Leave for 3 minutes or so, drain, and the skins can be peeled off easily. Cut the tomatoes into small pieces, removing as much of the seeds and leftover skins as possible. Discard as much juice as you can, using it for other things, and place all the ingredients into a large pan along with the vinegar and bouquet garni and simmer for about 30 minutes. At this stage force the mush through a sieve and discard the bouquet garni.

Return the mix to the heat and simmer gently for at least another 30 minutes to thicken the sauce. As long as you continue to stir you will find this process can create quite a thick product.

Pour the hot sauce into clean bottles/jars, carefully placing the lids/seals while the sauce is still boiling and then allow them to cool which will create a vacuum, thus preserving the contents.

Brown Sauce

In the UK we have a history of both plum sauce and apple sauce and some wonderful person joined them together to make chop sauce. This was flavoured with all sorts of spices and became Parliament Sauce, eventually reduced to the name HP sauce.

This recipe is not brown in itself, but is a sort of red colour. You can add treacle instead of the sugar, but this gives a slightly burned flavour.

Precycle!

You Will Need:

1.5kg (3lb) chopped apples
1.5kg (3lb) chopped plums
2 onions
5 cloves of garlic
50g (2oz) salt
500g (1.25lb) brown sugar
1.5 litres (2.5 pints) malt vinegar
2 tsps each of ginger, allspice and nutmeg
1 tsp cayenne pepper

Finely chop the onions and garlic and add to a large pan (not aluminium). Add the fruit and boil to a mush in the vinegar. This needs to be puréed as much as possible by passing through a sieve. I prefer this method of puréeing rather than simply 'wazzing' it in a food processor, but this step is up to you.

The sauce is not going to look like the bottle you buy from the shops but it will be superior to it in every way. You can core the apples if you wish but don't worry too much if some gets through. Return it to the pan and reduce on a low heat. Add the spices and mix well.

When it has reached the thickness and consistency you like, pour it into sterile containers. You will need to experiment with the salt content and also the sugar.

Peanut butter

Peanuts are full of oil and you can press them to get this oil out. Unfortunately you will need a hot climate to grow your own peanuts and for most of us it is difficult to get enough of them to make peanut oil. However, it really is easy. All you do is break them up with a hammer and then squash them with a cheese press through a couple of layers of muslin. You are best to soak the muslin in oil first and then leave them for a few days to drip away, increasing the pressure daily.

Peanut butter is much easier still. All you are doing is whizzing the peanuts in a food processor with a couple of tablespoons of oil (sunflower will do) per 150–200g of peanuts. The actual amount of oil will vary according to how much oil is in the peanuts, so you will have to experiment and make the consistency that suits you.

You can add salt for the sake of preserving as well as for flavour. If you want the butter to be crunchy then save a few peanuts from the processor and add them at the end. If you want to get rid of any pent up aggression wrap them in a cloth and bash them with a rolling pin. (It's up to you who you think about whilst bashing.)

You can make some pretty exotic peanut butters. Try adding hazel nuts, beech nuts or almonds but don't add acorns or you'll get a really bad tummy ache.

Yeast Extract

This was made in the English Midlands when an Edwardian brewer decided to try to sell the yeast that collected at the bottom of his tanks. There are several recipes but you have to collect the yeast from a brewing session. If you have made 5 gallons of beer, collect the yeast at the bottom of the barrel and get it into a pan excluding as much wort as possible. Bring this horrid looking sludge to the boil and add a teaspoon of salt for every half pint.

Boil for at least 15 minutes and then add a tablespoon of molasses for every half pint too.

The salt breaks down the yeast cell walls and the flavours develop as the contents of those cells spill out into the mixture.

You might love or hate yeast extract, and just as truly,

Precycle!

you might love or hate this recipe, but you'll never know unless you try.

Nutty/Chocolatey Type Spread

This was invented in the 1940s and takes advantage of the fact that many nuts are very similar to chocolate. In France, in particular, there is a tradition of using fruits of the forest and field in everyday products for the sake of frugality. French coffee, which in my opinion is hardly drinkable, contains a lot of chicory.

Nutella was created as a way of making chocolate go a whole lot further, and it is very easy to make.

You Will Need:

400g (13oz) hazel nuts
200g (6½ oz) caster Sugar
50g (2oz) cocoa powder

Put the nuts in the oven and cook them at 180°C (350°F, Gas mark 4) for 20 minutes. Give them a turn every five minutes to ensure even cooking. Allow them to cool on a tray and then remove the shells.

Put the nuts into a food processor and whizz away until they stick together. Do not stop. Continue the processing until the oil starts to seep out of the mixture. Then add all the other ingredients and transfer the completely mixed material to a sterile jar.

We eat it much more quickly than you have to worry about it keeping, as long as it is stored in the fridge. Some recipes say add a teaspoon of vanilla extract, but I never do.

Mint sauce

Mint is easy to grow but can become intrusive. Grow it in a pot, free standing, or even bury the pot with the plant in it under the soil to stop it from spreading all over your garden. Mint sauce is a simple thing to make and it only takes twenty minutes to make a large quantity.

You Will Need:

100g (3oz) mint, finely chopped both ways so you
effectively have small diamonds.
175g (6oz) sugar – white is best
250ml (half a pint) of white vinegar
3g (half a level tsp) salt

Bring the vinegar to the boil and slowly add the sugar, stirring all the time and then the salt. When all the sugar has dissolved, remove from the heat and add the mint, stirring in well and making sure it is evenly distributed. Bring to the boil, allow to cool and then bottle.

Mayonnaise

Mayonnaise is one of those magical sauces that we all buy but could make quite easily with eggs, oil and a whisk or a food processor. Needless to say, you can make better tasting mayo than you would ever get in the shops and if you keep your own hens this is one of the best ways to deal with a glut of eggs.

The important thing is that everything has to be at room temperature. Wash your bowl in hot water and dry it and all the utensils. If anything is cold the mayo will split and the whole thing will be a disaster.

Mayo is made from raw egg yolks, so make sure you know their status with regard to bacterial infections. It is,

Precycle!

of course, always better to use fresh eggs than old ones. Remember that the eggs you buy in the supermarket can be anything up to a month old.

This recipe (and there are many out there) uses a food processor, but you can use a hand whisk and beat the hell out of it.

You Will Need:

4 egg yolks
½ level tsp of English mustard
a pinch of salt and pepper
the juice of 1 lemon
330ml (2/3 pint) oil

Add all the ingredients except the oil to the food processor and whizz for 15 seconds. Drizzle in the oil very slowly.

Use light oils such as corn, peanut or sunflower oil. Olive oil will be more flavoursome and, it has to be said, gives a more yellow mayo.

Only add the oil in tiny amounts and don't add any more until the last bit has been completely incorporated. Taste for both saltiness and acidity. You might want to add a little more lemon.

Once you have made it you can chill the mayo and it will keep for the best part of a week in a sealed container.

Tartare Sauce

The very thing for fish and brilliant made fresh. In fact the stuff you buy is nothing like the real thing. Basically you are making a mayo, but adding so much more!

You Will Need:

4 egg yolks
1/2 level tsp of English mustard
a pinch of salt and pepper
the juice of 1 lemon
330ml (2/3 pint) oil
a peeled garlic clove
10g (1/2 oz) chopped fresh parsley
10g (1/2 oz) washed capers
4 baby gherkins

Make the mayo firstm, adding everything except the dry ingredients, then add the rest, pulsing the food processor to make a good mix of chopped ingredients.

Pickled Onions

The greatest part of September is dedicated to making the very finest pickles. Shallots are the best things to pickle but they can be so strong that you only need one and it will last for a week.

Pickling shallots marks this time of the year and hails on Christmas! Peel the shallots and place them in brine. This always makes me cry! The process removes a lot of water from the bulbs which will be partially replaced by vinegar.

You need to make a cold brine in which enough salt is dissolved in order for a raw egg to float. Peel your onions and/or shallots and cut out any bad flesh. Soak them overnight in the brine solution after which they should have shrunk a little.

Precycle!

The following day, boil up a mixture of vinegar and pickling spice, which you can buy ready made or you can prepare your own as follows:

You Will Need:

2 tbsps mustard seed
1 tbsp whole allspice
2 tsps black peppercorns
2 tsps whole cloves
1 tsp ground ginger
2 small bay leaves
5cm (2 inch) piece of cinnamon stick broken into small pieces

Mix all the ingredients and place in a sealed container. Leave for a week for the aromas to fuse. This can then be added to a litre (1.8 pints) of vinegar for pickling. You can, if you like, tie the spices in a muslin bag and soak it in the vinegar overnight (or for 2 days for a stronger brew). Some recipes ask you to boil the spices in the vinegar, which is just as good and fills the house with a lovely aroma.

You can also buy ready prepared pickling vinegar.

You can omit the spices if you wish. Strain the shallots from the brine and pop them into sterilised jars and cover them with very hot vinegar. Seal and leave until you are ready to consume. They should be left for at least a month. The flavour intensifies with time.

Ploughman's Pickle

This recipe is pretty close to the ploughman's pickle we all love. It is fairly easy to prepare and really does have that tang. You can replace some of the ingredients depending on what you have available, but the dates, apples and sugar are all really important.

You Will Need:

250g (10oz) peeled carrots chopped into 5mm (¼in) cubes
1 medium peeled swede chopped into 5mm (¼in) cubes
4-5 garlic cloves, peeled and finely chopped or grated
125g (4oz) dates, very finely chopped
2 onions peeled and finely chopped
2 medium apples chopped into 5mm (1/4in) cubes
15 small gherkins chopped into 5mm (1/4in) cubes
250g (10oz) dark brown sugar
1 tsp salt
4 tbsps lemon juice
500ml (¾ pint) malt vinegar
2 tsps mustard seeds
2 tsps ground allspice

Combine all the ingredients in a large pan and bring slowly to the boil, making sure that everything is completely mixed. When the pickle is boiling, reduce the heat so that it is just simmering and maintain this temperature for about 2 hours, stirring every few minutes or so to make sure the bottom of the pan doesn't catch and the pickle remains well mixed. You can add a little water if the mixture is becoming too thick.

When the vegetables are just becoming soft, spoon the pickle into sterile jars. Leave for at least a week to ensure that the flavours develop to make the familiar ploughman's flavour.

Precycle!

Piccalilli

This is the north of England's historic pickle which, particularly in Yorkshire, it is traditional to eat with bacon and eggs, and more or less everything! There are plenty of variations, but real piccalilli always has plenty of cauliflower in it.

You Will Need:

2.5kg (5.5lb) vegetables (cauliflower sprigs, baby onions, cucumber or gherkin)
1 litre (2 pints approx.) white vinegar
160g (5oz) sugar
25g (1oz) dry English mustard
25g (1oz) ground ginger
15g (½oz) turmeric
1 tbsp corn flour

Clean and peel all the vegetables you want to peel.

Make a brine by dissolving sugar in water so that a raw egg floats in it. Soak the vegetables, chopped to your required size, for 24 hours, then drain and dry them. Place most of the vinegar (keep about 2 tablespoons aside), the sugar and spices into a large saucepan and heat gently until the sugar has dissolved.

Add the vegetables and simmer gently until they are crisp on the outside but still soft inside. Make a paste with the corn flour and the remaining vinegar and stir it into the pickle. Bring the liquid to the boil, stirring all the time. Simmer for about 3 minutes, then remove from the heat. Bottle in sterile containers. The longer you can leave this pickle the better it will taste.

BBQ Sauce

A simple sauce for making other BBQ recipes. This isn't the type of sauce you would pour from a bottle onto a sandwich, but it can be used as a dip or a marinade.

You Will Need:

2 tbsps sunflower oil
1 large finely chopped onion
1 tbsp tomato purée or 2 tbsps of ketchup (as made above)
2 tbsps brown sugar
1 large tsp mustard powder
2 tbsps Worcestershire sauce or 2 tbsps of the above HP sauce recipe
150ml (5fl oz) water

Heat the oil and cook the onions to a slight translucence. You can add some garlic if you like. Add the other ingredients, except the tomato, which should be added last and beaten well in to the mixture.

This mixture contains no salt, but you can make a storing sauce if you add ½ a level teaspoon of salt and force the sauce through a sieve. It will keep for a week or two if stored in sterile containers in the fridge.

Baked Beans

There are so many recipes for baked beans that you will never want to buy them again. It is baked beans that show the difference between the value of money - a tin in the UK costing much less than it does to make the product - and the amount of environmental damage it takes to make it. Anyway, on to beans recipes.

The majority of baked beans are made from haricot

Precycle!

beans and you can buy them by the bagful which will last for ages. The basic idea is to create a tomato sauce that you bake the beans in, so that the flavours infuse across the whole dish. The following recipe calls for a kilo of haricots.

You Will Need:

1kg (2.2lbs) dried haricot beans, soaked overnight in water
25 tomatoes, finely chopped
4 leeks or red onions
8 tsps of sugar
1 tbsp of olive oil
400ml (⅔ pint) passata
Salt and pepper to taste

Soak the beans in water overnight. This will plump them up and make them soft. Put the beans, tomatoes, onions and olive oil into an ovenproof dish. Cover with the passata and add the sugar, salt and pepper. Stir and bake at 160°C (325°F gas mark 3) for 30 minutes. Stir again and bake for another 30 minutes or until tender.

You might produce 2 kilos of product and this can be frozen in dishes ready for heating up, or you can bottle them in kilner jars. If you buy bottled passata with a wide neck you can use these to bottle your beans.

Your Own Relishes

You can use the piccalilli recipe to make your own recipes. This is simple as long as you stick to the same process. Firstly the vegetables are brined overnight, secondly they are cooked until soft in sweet vinegar and finally they are thickened, if necessary. As long as you stick to the basic preserving mix of 1 litre (2 pints approx.) white vinegar to 160g (6oz) sugar, which is enough to preserve around 2.5kg (5lb) of vegetables, everything should be fine. Finally the mixture is thickened with corn flour, if necessary.

So hamburger relish would have equal amounts of tomatoes, cabbage, red peppers and onions. Onion marmalade would be nearly all onions and sweetcorn relish would be nearly all corn. You have to remember that many vegetables have a reasonably large water content, so things like onions should be brined for half a day longer to draw out that little extra liquid.

Most relishes will keep well in sterile jars, but once opened they need to be refrigerated and consumed within a month. The only other rule is that they taste better the longer they are allowed to keep before opening.

How to Make Various Jams

It is quite remarkable how people have forgotten how to make jam. In all of my years from childhood I never saw my mother make it. Jam was something you bought from the shop and, when supermarkets took over, jam making was set on the back shelf. It's not the jam we are missing out on, it is the knowledge of how to do it that we have lost.

In truth, I was given the opinion, perhaps passively and unintentionally, that other people's homemade jam was somehow inferior and not for eating. I was actually in my twenties before I encountered anyone making their own jam.

When making jam, have all your ingredients and utensils ready for use to stop you from panicking whilst actually cooking the jam.

When making strawberry jam you have to remember that this fruit contains very little pectin, the ingredient that causes the jam to set. So you need to add this in another way. You can extract it from other fruit high in pectin, such as gooseberries, but this can be a long process. You could also use lemons, particularly the pith, as they contain high levels of pectin, enabling your jam to set. But the easiest way is to buy a sachet of pectin and use that. I have used a Silver Spoon pectin sachet in the following recipe. These are readily available in the supermarket in the sugar section.

This book is not a treatise on jams and preserves, but I've included a couple of recipes to get the basics sorted, and from here you can then refer to the many books on the topic. You can use these methods to create any jam or preserve of any sort and, as always, there are plenty of techniques and lots of equipment to buy, should you wish to, but this recipe is easy enough to do in a single pan with little additional equipment.

Easy Strawberry Jam

You Will Need:

900g (2lb) strawberries
900g (2lb) white granulated sugar
1 sachet pectin
a knob of butter

Place your strawberries in a large pan and crush them with a potato masher. Leave a little whole fruit but gently squash them to release the juice. Warm the fruit on a low heat and add the sugar and the pectin.

Heat the mixture gently, stirring all the time until the sugar dissolves. You can tell when this has happened by looking at the mixture on the back of the spoon until you can't see any sugar crystals. Then turn up the heat and bring to the boil, stirring all the time.

Add the knob of butter; this will get rid of any scum which has formed on the top and once the jam reaches a rolling boil, continue to boil for four minutes.

After the four minutes is up, test a little of the jam on a cold plate or saucer. If it wrinkles and keeps its shape it is ready to bottle. If it is still runny then continue to boil it for a further 30 seconds and repeat the test. This may be a good time to use a thermometer to test for the temperature of the jam – if it has reached 104°C (220°F) it should be ready. Take off the heat and allow to cool for about five minutes before ladling it into jars.

Place your jam funnel in a sterilised jar and ladle the jam into the jar until it reaches the top. Then place a waxed disc over the surface of the jam. Place the lid on the jam straight away to keep it from spoiling in the air. If your lids are secure and airtight you don't really need to use a waxed disc but if you are using dustcover-type lids then a waxed disc is necessary. I prefer to use them because they protect the jam from moulding.

Label and date your jam and enjoy.

Microwave Marmalade

This is very easy to make and gives quick results. You can't really make it in large batches, but it's great if you only want a couple of jars of marmalade. You obviously need a microwave to make this type of preserve, but the results are great. Testing your marmalade for the setting point is very easy and can be done without a thermometer. Simply have a cold saucer at hand and place a little of the mixture on the plate. Allow it to cool for a few seconds then drag the handle end of the spoon through the centre. If it stays put it is ready but if it slips back together cook it for a further five minutes. This makes two 450g (1lb) jars of marmalade.

Precycle!

2 medium sized oranges
1 lemon
500g (1lb) sugar (I have tried it with jam sugar and ordinary
and find both work equally well)
500ml (1 pint) water

Squeeze the lemon into a large bowl that fits in your microwave. Cut the oranges into small pieces and place them in the bowl with the lemon juice.

Put all the pips and lemon peel into a muslin bag and put it in the centre of the bowl.

Pour over 300ml (12oz) of boiling water and soak for one hour.

Chop the orange peel as finely as you wish. Fine will cook quicker than thicker peel. Place it in the bowl and add the remaining 200ml (8oz) of boiling water. Then microwave on high for 15–20 minutes, stirring occasionally. Test the peel for tenderness and cook for a further five minutes if necessary.

Stir in the sugar until it is dissolved and microwave on high for ten minutes, watching to prevent the mixture from boiling over. Stir well and continue cooking for a further 15 minutes, stirring and testing for the setting point every five minutes.

Leave for ten minutes then ladle the mixture into clean jars and seal with a silicone paper disc and lid.

If you have any marmalade left, fill some clean ramekin dishes and store it in the fridge. Use this up first before the jars.

Herb Vinegar

Herb vinegars actually change the way you cook. It is a great way of saving the herbs and incorporating their flavours into your cooking.

Always use good quality vinegar. White and red wine vinegars are probably the best, and don't be tempted to use malt vinegar. These also make great presents and if you can get hold of some good clear bottles with a cork stopper you can create some fantastic gifts. All you have to do to make it look finished is to cover the cork and the top of the bottle with sealing wax.

You can use bamboo skewers to soak things like garlic cloves in the vinegar as well as making a decorative effect. Always use fresh herbs and spices, not powdered, because this will only make the vinegar cloudy, as will storing the vinegar in sunlight. All you have to do is to set the herbs into the bottle and then fill with vinegar. You will invariably need to top up the bottle because the herbs will absorb the liquid, especially if the filling is onion or garlic.

Most herbs can be washed and patted dry and that's enough. Spring onions can be trimmed and dipped for a few seconds into boiling water. Garlic needs to be peeled and dipped in the same way.

You can combine anything really. Remember, this is a work of art as well as something to cook with. But start with the obvious herbs; parsley, sage, rosemary, thyme. tarragon and garlic. Spear the garlic cloves with a bamboo skewer and use the skewer to set the herbs into position. Parsley is a great one to finish the filling because it fills the neck of the bottle and effectively acts as a sieve. Finally, add the vinegar.

Precycle!

How to Make Vinegar

One microbe (yeast) converts sugar into alcohol and another (bacteria) converts alcohol to acetate, which is the basis of vinegar. You can make your own vinegar by fermenting some sugar laden material to alcohol and then leaving this product open to the air to allow air borne bacteria to convert this to vinegar.

Let us say that you have made some cider and have completely removed the lees and then placed this in a sterile bucket. Cover the top of the bucket with a single muslin sheet and secure it with either string or tape. The bacteria will make its way inside and after about a month you will have the beginnings of cider vinegar. Taste the vinegar daily until you are happy with your product. You can then stop the process by putting it in a pan and bringing it to the boil, which will kill the bacteria. Allow it to cool naturally and then put it in sterile bottles.

In this way you can make any kind of vinegar. This is a perfect reason for brewing, even if you do not drink alcohol yourself. See the brewing chapter for all the kinds of brewing you can make vinegar from.

The Meat Counter

All Sorts of Meat, Pies, Bacon and Patés

I have to keep remembering that this is not a cook book. Well, it is actually, but it doesn't attempt to give you lots of different recipes for foods that are probably better covered elsewhere. The central remit of this book is to provide simple alternatives for every day basic foods and materials that we buy from the shops. For me there has to be a number of fundamental reasons for making as opposed to buying. It is perhaps best to illustrate the reasons by looking at a pork pie. I can make a pork pie and the recipe is included in this section. The sides will not be straight and the meat filling will not always be uniform. It might be an odd weight and sometimes will have thick jelly and other times runny. I can buy a pork pie from the shop, every day for a year if I like, and each one will be exactly the same. Made by a machine, each pie will have no soul. It will be mean and made for pennies with profit, not people, in mind. There is nothing wrong with profit but that's not the point. The machines that make the pies have only one object; to carry out their task with no alteration regardless of the subtle nuances of the ingredients. They are mean pies. My pie is not mean. Sure, I cannot always guarantee how it

Precycle!

comes out, but the pie is made by my hands, changing the manufacture as each pie is made.

Then, of course, I know what goes into my pie. It is simple. I don't have to eat chemicals designed simply to keep the pie looking good on a shelf. My pies never last that long! They are free from all the chemistry of the supermarket.

Finally, and obviously, my children eat my pies and they love them. I bet your children would too if you made them. The point is that the best seasoning for food is the pride of being homemade, the pride that you made it yourself. You can then be your own worst critic and strive to make a better one next time. And if all that isn't enough reason for you to make your own food, go to the supermarket and buy if you must.

You might currently be working all day to make the money you need to spend in the supermarket and to pay the bills. To make your own food, all of it, takes a great deal of time and this is in short supply in this crazy world. I can only tell you of my experience and hope you might have the same. You see we can fill our days with many things; work, ambition, money making, business, family and the search for fulfilment. I personally have found life to have greater meaning, more pleasure, and a greater connection with my family as well as (for some strange reason I imagine this whenever I do it) my history when I make bread of any kind – chapatti in particular. There is something solemn about adding water to flour and creating a really tasty bread – just that, flour and water and nothing else, save a little salt. This same process has been the mainstay of human life for tens of thousands of years, and boy – that's some connection!

For me the argument is not about how on earth can I find enough time to make my own food basics, it is about personal wealth. I am enriched by the knowledge of making my own, the experience of making my own and especially by the eating of what I have made. How many people know how to make a pork pie (or any other pie, for that matter)? But I do, and that makes me rich. I might not be able to afford to buy the most expensive pie in the shop, but believe me, no money in the world could buy a pie like mine – or yours, if you choose to make it.

One last point, and it strongly depends on the previous one. You are not looking to make food that is as good as the food you can buy in the shops. You are looking to make food that is its superior in every respect.

Confit

A confit is a preserved dish. In fact the word means "to preserve." The idea is to cook the meat for a long time so that the bone is cooked too. Then the flesh is forked off, put into a sterile dish and very hot fat is poured on top. Now you have a dish of fat with meat in it, which is allowed to cool. The confit will keep for a fortnight. Actually it will last a month, but it's always best to be on the safe side.

The best fat to use is goose or duck. Lard is not quite so useful because it has a tendency to leak water into the food, increasing the chances of spoilage. Goose fat in confit coats completely. Simply heat it until it is quite hot and then pour it onto the shredded meat. You can make a confit from pork, lamb, rabbit, chicken or anything. The secret is to do everything hot, then allow it to cool slowly before putting the confit in the fridge.

To serve the fat can be heated so it runs off the meat or you can simply scrape it off.

Precycle!

Terrine

It is only a short step from a confit to a terrine. Here the meat is cooked with salt added and packed into a dish. Terrines are covered in salted jelly and can last for around six weeks. This is because they are salted. They are more palatable than a confit because no fat is used.

Jelly is made by cooking bones for a long time. Pig's trotters are good. Simply cover them with water and boil them for an hour, making sure they are only just covered. Strain the liquid and simmer it until it is reduced by half. Add 1tsp of salt for every 500ml of liquid. When it is cold this liquid will set hard. You can melt it again by using a bain marie.

Since the terrine is salted and in a block, it is a good way of preserving offal. The earliest pate was made of pounded lung, liver, pancreas and testes. The flavour of poultry liver will disguise the more horrid things and consequently pate has become synonymous with the flavour of chicken, duck or goose liver.

A Simple Pate Recipe

You Will Need:

500g (1lb) chicken livers well washed
125ml (¼ pint) chicken stock
1 large onion very finely chopped
2 stalks of celery cut finely
2 grated garlic cloves
3 crushed peppercorns
7g salt (1 heaped tsp)
a generous tsp Dijon mustard
50ml (1½fl oz) brandy
50g (2oz) butter

-46-

Sweat the onionsin a little oil and then the garlic until very soft and translucent, but not brown. Add the stock and the celery then the livers and, as they are cooked, add all the other ingredients, except the butter and half the brandy.

TIP: Add half the salt, taste and add a proportion of the rest, depending on the flavour. Remember, the salt is there to preserve, but who wants to eat pate that is too salty?

Mix thoroughly while cooking and finally transfer to a blender and beat until smooth.

Heat an earthenware pot in the oven to sterilise it and add the pate. Pour over the rest of the brandy and allow the dish to cool. When cool, melt the butter and pour it over the pate as a seal.

This will keep for at least ten days in the fridge, but eat within two days once opened.

Curing

There are two ways of chemically killing bacteria in food. The process is known as curing. The first way is to use a poison, such as saltpetre. This chemical interacts with bacteria and kills them in ways that are pretty safe for humans to eat afterwards (assuming you only use a small amount).

Secondly, you can take away enough water to create an environment that slows the growth of bacteria almost to a standstill. This is not poisoning the bacteria. Nothing can live without water and a high concentration of salt stops bacterial growth. In effect you are tearing the microbes apart by forcing the water out of their tissues. There are two substances that will do this, salt and sugar. For meat and fish we tend to use salt. For fruit we use sugar, sometimes in the form of honey.

Sometimes we use vinegar as a preserving agent for fish. This is only ever done in conjunction with salt, which remains the major preserver in the mix.

Best of all, for liquid food we use alcohol, but that's another story altogether!

All commercially preserved food uses both salt and saltpetre as a preservative. Any food that is to be preserved and sold has to contain a minimum amount of saltpetre; 5g per kilo. This is very difficult to mix properly if you are only producing a small amount of cure.

However, it is possible to cure at home without saltpetre, so long as you are sure you have added enough salt! Curing is a payoff. On the one hand there is the obvious danger of eating bad meat. You may die in hours. On the other are the obvious problems of having too much salt in the diet. Well, in its defence salt will keep you alive and if for some reason you cannot freeze your meat, what else can you do? It is important that people know how to cure with salt.

Making a Cure

Curing Salt

Curing salt is not the same as cooking or kitchen salt. What is often sold as curing salt is a variation of a substance known as Prague Powder. This is a pre-mixed concoction of saltpetre and kitchen salt. Another quicker acting version of Prague Powder (Known as Prague Powder #2) contains sodium nitrate.

Use curing salt for anything that is thick, such as a ham

or a big piece of meat you need to keep for a long time, or will be given or sold to others. Use ordinary kitchen salt when you do not need to keep the product or you eat a lot of the stuff and it will not be kept for a long time, such as bacon.

Sugar, either white or brown, is a fundamental part of the cure and the darker the colour, the smokier and richer the mix. Honey and molasses are also used for hams and bacon and not just for the cure. Spices and peppers of all kinds are called for in various recipes including things like garlic salt. You do not need to worry about the salt content of these because they are only used in small quantities.

Do the Egg Test

When you add salt to water it dissolves, as we all know. If you put an un-boiled egg into water it will sink, but if you keep on dissolving salt in the water it will eventually float. When the egg floats it just happens to be exactly the right concentration for curing.

Boiled or Roast Ham

A boiled ham, or sandwich ham, is easy to make and this recipe calls for pickling spice, which is easily made at home from this generic recipe. I tend to leave out the cloves because they remind me of the dentist.

You Will Need:

2 bay leaves
2 tbsps mustard seed
2 tsps black peppercorns
2 tsps whole cloves
1 tbsp allspice
1 tsp ground ginger

Precycle!

1 tsp cardamom seeds
1 cinnamon stick

Give them a good crack with the pestle so that the cinnamon stick can be handled with a spoon and the flavours leach out, and store in an airtight container.

The cure makes a gallon, or 4.5 litres, and you do not need all of this for a ham, so you will need a good sealable container for the excess cure mix.

The essential ingredient is curing salt – with nitrate and nitrite.

Curing Salt

You Will Need:

1kg (2,2lbs)curing salt
4.5 litres (1 gallon) water
125g (4oz) sugar
1 tbsp of the pickling spice described above

The meat is probably best as a lean pork loin, or a boned leg. It would always be preferable if you could buy from a proper butcher who can guarantee that the meat has not previously been frozen.

Cool the cure by keeping it in a cold fridge overnight. I use a plastic bucket with a sealable lid in which to do the curing, which takes around 5 days. Do keep the brine in a cool place throughout the process and you can, if you wish, inject the cure into the centre of the meat to ensure its penetration throughout.

Once this is complete it is time to cook your ham. There are a number of recipes for this. Some place the ham in boiling water and cook for an hour or you can cook it in the oven in water or roast it with a honey topping.

In all cooking of cured meat products I would advocate the use of a meat thermometer which will confirm that the centre of the meat has been heated to 75°C for at least 15 minutes.

Bacon

There is no reason for you to ever buy bacon because it is so simple to create a meat that is far superior to the shop bought product, and for far less money. You might well be surprised to know that you can make bacon at home. It might be an even greater surprise to hear that you can make bacon overnight and an even greater surprise that you can make and enjoy bacon that is not only great to taste, but good for the heart!

Bacon is made by machine. Wet cure is where the meat is soaked in a very strong brine solution. This is not as bad as people imagine because the bacon actually loses water in the curing process. Injected cure bacon is where a solution of salt and nitrite is injected into the meat to ensure the deep core of muscle gets sufficient curing chemicals, making it safe from spoilage. This is the cheapest way of making bacon and you can tell when the scum comes out of the meat and the bacon shrivels to almost nothing.

The amount of nitrite added (also known as saltpetre) is strictly controlled and has been a subject for health scares, especially in America. The bacon you can make at home uses none whatsoever. It is used as a double defence against spoilage and commercially cured products have to use it by law. The foremost reason why manufacturers use, though, is because it keeps the meat pink. For some reason people prefer pink bacon and sausages, and this is enhanced by nitrite. The real colour of the meat is a somewhat more greyish hue.

Precycle!

Basic Green Bacon Cure

OK, the name is off-putting, but I can assure you this bacon is not green, but it isn't pink either! Green bacon cure has no saltpetre, it is simply a mixture of salt and sugar: at least 70% salt. You can flavour this with various additions.

To make a kilo (just over 2lb) you will need 700g (25oz) salt and 290g (10oz) sugar. The rest is made up of flavours. Of course you can add flavour by using different types of sugar and these are some that have worked for me. Choose any combination you like, but do make sure that the additions in total represent no more than 5% of the mixture by weight.

You Will Need:

a finely chopped bay leaf (up to 1% of the total weight)
finely chopped rosemary (up to 3% of the total weight)
pepper (up to 1% of the final weight)
mustard (up to 1% of the final weight)
finely chopped mint (up to 2% of the total weight)

Of course you can vary the type of cure by changing the type of sugar you use. Using thick brown sugar will give a completely different flavour from refined white sugar. I usually give the coarse sugars a quick grinding in the pestle and mortar in an attempt to get all the crystals roughly the same size.

The 'Rub it in' Method of Making Bacon

This way you simply take enough of your cure to generously cover just the meat and rub it in all over. Be quite vigorous with this process and make the cure penetrate the flesh. Once it has been well rubbed, place in a dish, which you seal with clingfilm and leave overnight. In the morning you will need to pour off the liquor and repeat the process. Repeat this for 5 days, after which both the skin of the pork and the meat itself will have changed consistency. You should now test your bacon by frying a little and tasting it.

Ultra Low Salt Bacon

Basically, the bacon you buy is anything up to 3% salt content. But salt doesn't penetrate the fatty meat, so you can devise a way of getting the salt directly to the meat where you need it. What follows is very easy and based on 1 kilo (2.2lbs) of pork. All you have to do is get the butcher to slice whatever pork meat you like as though it was bacon. Then the fun starts.

Spread the slices on a tray and weigh out the amount of salt you will require. Add sugar to make up the cure. Now you can make ultra low salt bacon! Healthy bacon! The cure is made up of equal amounts of salt and sugar. The ingredients here make a kilo of bacon.

You Will Need:

5g or 1 level tsp of salt will make very mild bacon
10g or 2 level tsps will give a mild flavour but will certainly smell like bacon when cooking
15g or 3 level tsps is very definitely bacon, and is still only half the commercial salt content or 1.5% salt and thus qualifies for the title 'healthy bacon!'

Don't forget that you are adding equal amounts of salt and sugar, mixing it up and sprinkling it, but only on the meat, not the fat. Keep it covered and store it in the fridge overnight.

I have also found that with very low salt bacon if you pile the slices on top of each other, the underside of the slice above benefits from the salt on the slice below.

Some people get a shock when they taste sweet cure bacon. It is surprising that shop bought bacon (and sausages too, for that matter!) contains a lot of sugar in order to disguise the saltiness. So start with a saltier cure and gradually work your way down. Even if you make bacon that has 20g of salt per kilo, this is still a saving of 13g on the very healthiest bacon the shops have to offer. This bacon doesn't keep as well as shop bought, but it will freeze and last for months. Clearly the higher the saltcontent, the longer it will last, but if you treat the product like cooked meat then you will not go far wrong.

This bacon is brilliant in pasta sauces as well as all manner of more traditional methods of serving. It also makes a wonderful layered pie with pork and other meats.

Pork Pie

This is a recipe for a pork pie. Now I know you will call me a cheat as everything is bought, but you have to start somewhere and there are plenty of people who have never ever made a pork pie. Now here is a promise: this pie will knock your socks off! It is the simplest recipe you can possibly make and does use shop bought pastry, but it could just as easily be a chicken pie or a pork and 'something else' pie. Just use it as the basis for whatever kind of pie takes your fancy and experiment with the limitless options.

Please be aware that this is a luxury pork pie and they cost a small fortune in the shops!

You Will Need:

500g (1.1lb) prime minced pork
350g (12oz) belly pork
445g (1lb) pork shoulder
500g (1.1lb) shortcrust pastry
(if you make your pastry with a strong bread flour it will
maintain the shape better)

First mince the Belly pork. It is rich in fat and has great skin. Put it in the food processor or mincer and whizz it into a paste. This will add great flavour. The fat, skin and meat will form a light paste.

Cut the shoulder into large chunks so that you get a variation in texture in the finished pie. Put all the meat together into the same bowl and add seasoning, mixing it in thoroughly.

Bought pies have 3% salt. For a pie of this type this would mean eight teaspoons of salt and an amount of saltpetre. Add 3 level teaspoons or 15g of salt. This is approximately 1% salt. You can also add half a teaspoon of pepper and maybe some mustard, mace and other herbs. You should perhaps start simple and add just the salt first. Whatever you choose to add, mix it in well so that all the seasoning is completely even across the pie.

Roll out 80% of your pastry and put it into a baking tin. I use silicone trays because they don't need greasing. If you use a proper tin, grease it first.

Fill the cavity with your meat mixture and press it down, filling it to the very brim and forcing it down with your hands. Then roll out the Lid

Put the lid on and crimp it in place all round with a fork. Make some steam holes in the lid and you can then

Precycle!

glaze it with an egg if you like. Tidy up the edges with a knife, the neater the better.

Cook in the oven for 90 minutes at 175°C (Gas mark 3). To test if the meat is cooked, carefully place a knife into the meat and leave it for a few seconds. If the knife is clean when removed the pie is ready. If there are some streaks on the knife then give it another 15 minutes.

Once you have made this you will want to experiment. Try making your own pastry. The above recipe uses short crust, but traditionally pork pies have been made from hot water crust pastry. Also bear in mind the tip about using strong bread flour in the recipe ingredients.

Hot Water Crust Pastry

You Will Need:

170g (6oz) flour
170ml (6fl oz) water
85g (3oz) lard
a pinch of salt

Put the flour into a bowl, add the salt and mix well. Put the water and lard into a pan and bring to the boil. Pour the mixture into the flour and mix rapidly with a wooden spoon. Use the pastry while it is warm. Wrap the hot water crust pastry around a jam jar (traditionally called a dolly and made out of wood). This will serve as an effective mould for a small, rustic looking pork pie

Jelly

You could use gelatine, but the real way is to buy pigs trotters (feet). Cover two of them with water in a pan and then simmer for two hours. You can add a little water if it begins to run dry. After two hours sieve the feet and bones out of the liquid and then reduce on the heat by half. As is cools down you can see how it jellifies. The same recipe and method can be used in all sorts of dishes, including your pie. Carefully pour the hot liquid through the steam hole and allow it to cool completely.

Pressed Ham

The most important thing to remember here is that everything (including yourself) should be scrupulously clean!

In the shops, pre-sliced ham costs anything from £12 to £20 per kilo. This is much tastier and will cost no more than £4 a kilo.

Boil two bacon hocks, ham shanks or whatever you call them where you live. If you boil them for over two hours all the fat will be rendered off. Keep the stock and dilute it by 50% with boiling water to reduce the salt. From this you need 500ml to make the jelly. You could use pig's trotters, boiled in the stock to make the jelly, but I found the resulting product looked a bit grey on the sandwich, so I used gelatine added to the hot diluted stock instead.

Remove the meat from the hocks, place it in a bowl and shred it with a fork. Press it down, fill the bowl with jelly and leave it to set.

I tried an alternative method which involved putting the meat in a cheese press to get a higher density product. I pressed it for a couple of hours and then stood it in jelly. You do get more meat than jelly, but the meat is slightly less well set. This doesn't really matter if you keep it in the fridge as it will stay together well enough to slice. This will last for three days, assuming that your family will give it the chance.

Precycle!

Pork and Chicken

Unsalted meat will not keep as well as cured, so you have to add a little. The process is much the, same but you have to measure the salt content. This way you are going to boil the meat, and then keep the stock piping hot.

Add the gelatine to the stock and then measure the appropriate amount of salt. For 500ml of stock you need to add a level teaspoon of salt (5g) for a 1% solution. Most cured food has 3% salt, so this is already a lower salt content. Of course, you can add less. The product's keeping qualities will, however, be reduced. I find that the jelly is very salty, but you are only using a fraction of this and when it mingles with the unsalted meat it is fine. You could even miss out the salt altogether and add it later to taste, if you wish.

Fill a dish with your cooked, shredded chicken or pork and press down hard. Then add the hot jelly stock to it, pressing down with a spoon and expelling as much air as possible. Continue this process until all the meat is covered with stock. Try to get as much meat in the dish as you can, pressing all the time. If you want a higher density product, really pack the meat in and press it down with a plate or any other implement that will fit.

Brawn

I was put off brawn when I saw a whisker inside a big jelly at the pork shop, but in essence what you have made is brawn, except this comes from a pig's head. It consists mainly of cheek muscle with some feet and various 'other bits' thrown in. The thing about brawn is that it sets itself because the bones and feet make great jelly. The problem with this is that it turns out a grey colour and you also have to make sure that the all the gruesome pieces (some far more disconcerting than whiskers!) are filtered out.

Variations

You can use more than one type of meat in a sandwich. Chicken and ham go together well. You can also bulk out the meat by adding a boiled egg. These recipes are quite different from paté, which can be bulked out with breadcrumbs or rusk, as in a sausage or pie mix.

Burgers

Everyone loves burgers. They have become a family staple, but the ones you buy from the supermarket freezer are a mere shadow of the real thing. These are nothing like the burgers you buy in the shops. We add nothing but some chopped mint to them, and have become so used to their slightly firmer texture. It's just like eating slightly spiced meat.

Buy the best minced steak you can find. You can use the cheapest mince, but incorporate 50g of breadcrumbs, too. This soaks up the excess fat, but you will still get a lot of residue. For every kilo you use, add 5g salt and a handful of finely chopped mint. The meat will not taste minty at all, but rather spicy.

I always shape the burgers with a ring cutter because they then usually stay flat all the way along the edge. If I use my hands they invariably seem to end up looking a little like torpedoes.

If you have invested in a grinding machine you can buy any cut of beef, cut it up and grind it after removing all of the bits you don't need in the mix. Home grinding is great because you can produce a product you wouldn't normally buy. If you have harsh, grainy meat such as

Precycle!

shin, you can grind it with large blades first of all and then re-grind the mince to make a much finer product that will cook easily.

Sausages

We are going to look at how to make a number of sausage recipes. Some of you will already know the fundamentals of the requirements for good sausage making, but we are going to skim over them for the benefits of any novices.

Sausage casings, made either from intestines or synthetic material, hold the sausage together. As the skin cooks it shrinks, improving the shape of the sausage and compressing the contents. The skin actually holds the flavour in the sausage and serves as a self-contained little oven, so it should definitely not be pricked. You can even make sausages without skins, and therefore without all the messing that stuffing involves.

If you want to try sausage making without buying any casings, ask your butcher for some caul. This is a fatty membrane found inside an animal and sold as a very thin sheet of tissue. Give it a quick rinse and use it to roll your mixture into. Pretend it is simply a sheet of cling film and simply roll your stuffing into a sausage shape, wrap it up and cook it. The caul all but disappears in the cooking process.

Fat

Fat melts during the cooking process, distributing heat evenly inside the sausage and cooking it from within. Low fat sausages are trickier to cook and usually less tasty. A good sausage will always have some fat in it and healthy sausages certainly contain some fat. A sausage is not intended for everyday eating and a well cooked sausage (because of the fat content) is far better than a partially cooked low fat sausage.

Water

Water is a vital ingredient in a sausage. Without water the meat will not stuff into the casings, but will fall apart. Sausages are succulent and much of this comes from the added water, which might be as much as 10% of the sausage weight.

Salt

When you make your own sausages you control the salt content. You can have ordinary salt at 3% or 6 level teaspoons per kilo, low salt at 1.5% or 3 level teaspoons per kilo or even no salt sausages. The latter will not keep long and will need to be cooked or frozen straight away.

Before you freeze your sausages, ask your butcher if the meat can be frozen. Some butchers sell nothing but previously frozen meat which is completely unsuitable for re-freezing.

Rusk or breadcrumbs

Rusk, breadcrumbs or cereal are an important part of a sausage. They bind the ingredients, soak up the cooking juices and help to improve the consistency. Although an essential component they add nothing to the flavour of the sausage.

Precycle!

A Basic Sausage Recipe

You Will Need:

1kg (2.2lbs) of pork shoulder
200g (6oz) sausage making rusk, or breadcrumbs if you prefer
200ml (6oz) water
1 tsp salt
½ tsp pepper
1 mixing bowl
1 grinder or food processor
1 sausage stuffer
at least 2 metres (6½ft) of hog casing

Hog casings are easiest to use for first-timers so I have included them for the recipe, but you can also use beef, sheep or vegetarian casings as required. You can buy sausage casings online, but you can also go to the butcher and ask him for some. He will even grind your meat for you if you tell him what you are doing.

In addition to the above you will also need a tray to collect the filling sausage casing as the mixture comes out of the stuffer and a knife to hand.

Open your packet of skins (ignoring the smell!) and place them in a bowl of clean water. Replace the water several times until the smell has gone away. Now rinse the skins under running water, both inside and out.

Chop your meat into centimetre cubes and then grind or mince them. If you have to use a food processor, pulse the machine to avoid it becoming like soup. Add your other ingredients to this mix, depending on the size of your food processor. Mix everything as thoroughly as you can and, once you have created your sausage mix, you are ready to stuff your casing. You can fry a small amount of the mixture to check that you are happy with the seasoning.

Stuffing

Most people will have a sausage extension to their food processor but I find that the easiest method is to use a hand cranked mincing machine that can be bought very cheaply. It doesn't stuff the sausage very quickly, but it does give you more control. Push the skin onto the stuffing tube and crank away. This will push the meat into the tube and pull the skin away as you go. Let the sausage come off the tube evenly by controlling the speed which can be done by varying the cranking.

You can link the sausages by simply twisting lots of times at regular intervals and then snipping through the twist with a sharp knife. Tie a knot in the open end of the skin.

Of course there are all kinds of recipes and variations you can make. Try adding some chopped sage to the mix as a first experiment. Another option might be to add some chopped apple, which is really tasty. There are an infinite number of variations you could try, limited only by imagination and taste. The following are a number of my own favourites which might whet your appetite.

Sweet Chilli Sausage

This is pure heaven. Instead of using water you simply add sweet chilli sauce to the pork mix. This opens the doors for all kinds of further Chinese type sausages.

You Will Need:

1kg (2.2lbs) pork shoulder

Precycle!

150g (5oz) breadcrumbs
125ml (¼ pint) sweet chilli sauce
1 heaped tsp salt
2 - 4 crushed and grated garlic cloves
2 metres (6½ft) of hog cashing

Simply grind the meat, add all the other ingredients together, mix well to make sure everything is incorporated and stuff into hog casing. You needn't bother with the chop sticks!

Mushroom Sausage

This should really be called a woodland sausage or September sausage. Mushrooms make great vegetarian sausages, but you have to be careful not to grind them too much. Indeed, you don't really need a grinder.

You Will Need:

1kg (2.2lbs) ssorted mushrooms
300g (10oz) white breadcrumbs
150ml (¼ pint) vegetable stock
50ml (1½fl oz) extra virgin olive oil
1 heaped tbsp salt
1 tbsp black pepper
the juice of 1 lemon
2 metres (6½ft) of thin vegetarian casing

Chop the mushrooms into small pieces. Some mushrooms blacken on chopping. Chop these more coarsely. Sprinkle the cut mushrooms with lemon juice, salt and pepper. Completely mix all the ingredients and stuff into the casing.

The Fish Counter

Fresh Fish and Shellfish

The sea is a fantastic resource. It is so productive that everyone could live off its bounty and the stocks of fish would still be safe. However, factory fishing and processing in ways that are unsustainable render the fish of the world increasingly sparse. Fish of all kinds have been used to feed cattle, poultry, pigs and all kinds of farm animal. For most of the products you buy on the shelves, fish have probably had a hand in their production.

However, if we caught our own fish and killed and gutted it ourselves, we would probably be doing fishkind a great service, as well as our families, for the great produce we would be bringing to the table.

In Europe, and much of the rest of the world, most of the fish consumed comes from the waters of the UK. The Spanish eat pilchards (and oh what lovely pilchards they are too!) They come from Devon. Italy is famous for its expensive Frito Misto and the herring, the squid and the whitebait all come from British waters.

Buy vongole in some Venetian restaurant and the cock-

Precycle!

les come from Morecambe Bay in Northwest England. Yet in England we turn our noses up at one of the greatest resources we have in this country. Shame on us!

This chapter is not going to teach you how to fish. It will just whet your appetite. All of those fish products you see on the shelves could cost you pennies if you caught the fish yourself but, failing that, get to know your fish market. It might mean getting up early, but it is worthwhile. But what better pastime than to spend the day looking at the sea, breathing clean air, or watching the world revolve around a dreamy river while you catch your dinner. But please be safe on the shore. Beaches are dangerous places, and the one which is the world's largest producer of cockles is also the most deadly.

If you are thinking about any sort of self-sufficiency, then a trip to the seaside should be at least a monthly occurrence. All you need is a little knowledge, a rod of almost any sort to bag some herring and a net to enable you to go shrimping.

Killing a Living Thing

It is not possible to live on the planet as a human and not kill, however innocently. However, if an animal dies for our food it should be respected, cared for, even loved. If it came to choosing between being crushed to death in a large net, condemned to suffocate slowly on the ice in pain or being bashed on the head by me and dead within seconds of being pulled from the water I feel confident that the fish would opt for the latter. I also use the whole of the fish; for human food, for oil,for pet food and finally rotted down for plant food. The same goes for any animal we consume. Use the whole animal and celebrate the great gift it has given you; its life for your benefit.

While we're on the subject, the same goes for chicken, eggs, pork and any meat you might care to cite. Use the carcass, make soup but don't throw anything away. In this way you will be living a greener and more connected life.

Mackerel

At almost any time of the year you can catch mackerel. You can catch them on feathers, which are shiny looking lures that you buy from the bait shop. They can have up to six hooks on them. You simply cast them out and then slowly pull them in. On most casts you will catch fish. You can stand on a rock at the beach and spend the whole day (or night) casting in the fresh air.

A Million Things To Do With a Herring

The song "You Shall Have a Fishy, On a Little Dishy" is testament to how the herring boats in the Northeast of England fed the population. One of the basic skills of the kitchen used to be gutting and filleting. People imagine this to be a messy job, but it really doesn't have to be. There are many ways of doing this and I find my own method works well.

Cut the dorsal fin from the fish's back with a pair of scissors. Then remove the heads behind the gills and also the tail. You will need a very sharp, stout knife for this.

Then, on the belly of the fish, insert the knife into what would have been the fish's bottom, with the blade facing outwards. Draw the knife all the way up the belly, dividing the fish into two. Repeat the manoeuvre, opening up the tail end. Because the head and tail have already been removed, the gut will fall out of the fish, especially if encouraged to do so with the thumb. Wash the inside under the cold tap.

Precycle!

To fillet the fish, cut along its back until you feel the backbone. Continue to draw the knife to one side of the backbone, paring away the flesh and leaving the bones behind. You will get the odd bone left in the fillet; these can easily be removed with a pair of tweezers. Repeat the process for the other half of the fish.

Once you have your fillets there are virtually limitless recipes for them. You can roll them up, pierce them with a cocktail stick and soak them in spiced, peppered vinegar, when they are called rollmops. You can coat them in seasoned oatmeal and fry them lightly in butter or finely grate garlic over fillets that have been brushed with a little olive oil and grill them for three minutes.

Herring Frito Misto

This is nothing more than a plate of fried fish with herring fillets as the major constituent. Include also sardines, whitebait and a good quality cod or haddock cut into reasonable sized cubes. Fry the fish individually and drain onto a kitchen towel. The whitebait can be fried by the handful. Place them in a plastic bag with a good tablespoon of seasoned flour, close the neck of the bag and lightly shake to incorporate both flour and fish. Empty the whitebait into your frying basket and carefully plunge them into extremely hot oil until golden brown. Serve all the fish together with a green salad and tartare sauce. Lovely!

Finally, try cooled grilled herring and garlic salad. Grill the fillets and, when cool, flake the meat into a dish, adding grated garlic and a dash of olive oil. Mash with a fork and season with pepper.

The coast is full of brilliant fish, from cod to eel. There are lots of ways to catch them and the very best way of finding out is by going fishing for herring and then chatting to the others that are there. Try fishing off a pier for dogfish.It is great fun and you do get lots of rock salmon. Sole and flatfish galore are in season all year round and, if you want a real experience, try a boat trip fishing off a wreck. The skipper will hire you any kit you need and will even gut the fish for you.

By the way, you don't have to salt white fish. They should stay fresh kept in a bit of ice until you get home,and then when you can freeze them properly.

Shellfish

Cockles live in large areas of mud flats on the sides of estuaries and on open sandy areas of the inter-tidal zone. They feed in shallow water and bury themselves under the surface when the tide goes out, which makes them relatively easy to rake up. If you are going to do this, however, watch out for fast incoming tides and quicksand and get as much information as you can about the area. If you go to some large estuarine beaches you will often find gangs of people working the patch. Explain to them that you are only scratching a bag full for personal use. You will be rewarded with friendly banter and some tips as to where the best places are.

Boil the cockles for a couple of minutes and then work out the flesh into a jar of vinegar. An hour's work should provide you with a month's worth of the best pizza toppings available and the very best steak and kidney pie additive.

Mussels are found on jetties and piers and attached to rocks. All you have to do is pull them off, but check first about the sewage status of the beach. They will keep fresh stored in a bit of ice or in one of those insulated picnic boxes with a couple of frozen bars inside.

Precycle!

Razor clams burrow vertically into the sand and leave breathing holes at the tops of their tunnels. You can see their indentations in the sand at low tide. All you have to do is pour a handful of salt on the hole and, in a few seconds, the clam will come flying out. Boil or steam them first which will kill them. Then treat the meat like scallop.

Limpets are brilliant cooked in wine and garlic and they make a brilliant sauce. It's a bit like eating the ocean. Take only the live ones but find out first which you have to catch carefully and do wear good boots. At low tide pour seawater over them and they will start to loosen. If they don't move, leave them. Alternatively, when the tide is in, give them a tap and they should tighten up to the rock. If the animal moves, kick it off the rock with your good boots.

Cook them quickly. Boil them first, remove them from their shells and then add them to your chosen dish in place of other molluscs.

Rules for Molluscs

To begin with there are some rules about preparing molluscs for eating. When you collect them they should be eaten as soon as possible. Any open shells should be discarded if, once tapped on the table, they remain so. Some molluscs hold themselves to rocks with strands of protein called beards. These should be pulled away to stop them spoiling the dish.

Scrub the shells in running water and, once cooked, any shell that remains closed should be discarded.

Mussels Marinière

This dish can be adapted, replacing mussels with anything available. The sauce tastes like concentrated seaside and, whereas we have used wine in this recipe, you could go mad and use brandy.

You Will Need:

a large finely chopped onion
30g (an ounce or a big knob) of butter
2 to 3 cloves of finely crushed garlic
15g (½ oz) flour
half a bottle of white wine
300ml (½ pint) double cream
800g (1lb 10oz)) mussels
chopped parsley

First melt the butter in a steep sided pan and sweat off the onions and garlic until they are translucent, after which you sprinkle the flour into the butter mix to thicken. Stir well to avoid lumps, and continue to cook for another three minutes.

Slowly add the wine, stirring all the time. Continue to stir until the sauce begins to thicken. Then add the mussels to the sauce, and shake the pan well to settle the contents. Cover immediately with a lid and turn up the heat. The wine is now steaming the mussels and this should take between 12 and 15 minutes to complete. Check the dish and stir every few minutes, replacing the lid each time.

When all the shells are open, turn down the heat and slowly add the cream, stirring and allowing the sauce to thicken. Finally, season and add a generous amount of parsley. Serve with freshly baked bread.

Precycle!

Collecting Edible Crabs and Shrimps

Almost everyone has loaded a crab line with pieces of bacon and pulled out a prickly little green beast no more than a few inches across and holding on for dear life with one of its claws, only to see it skittle across the sand and back into the sea.

There are two crabs found on our shores which are worth collecting for food. All the rest are either too small or too full of toxins because they prefer to eat near waste pipes. The edible crab is usually as big as a small dinner plate and has a sandy red body with black tips to the claws, and the spider crab looks pretty much like a large alien spider.

Edible crabs are usually collected by putting a little bait in a netted box into which the crab can climb, but cannot escape. The traps are quite cheap to buy and, if you have a boat to drop the net on the bottom of around twenty feet of water, you will be able to catch a crab a day for your dinner.

You can hunt both edible and spider crabs at low tide by lifting stones near the shoreline. They will not resist being collected and are quite safe to pick up from behind. Spider crabs congregate in large numbers at low tide in the winter in the southern counties of England and they are packed with good meat.

All crustaceans should, wherever possible, be narcotised before killing. This is done by placing them in the freezer for at least two hours. They can then be plunged into boiling water, where they will feel no pain and death will be instant.

Shrimping can still be done on all our shores where pollution levels are within safe limits. The basic tool is a push net, so called because you push it along. It is wide and sturdy and in the shape of a 'D'. The net is pushed along the floor of the sea at a depth of a foot or so and, after a short while, enough shrimps for a mouthful are easily collected and an afternoon's work should be enough for a good curry. But you will also catch other marine creatures, from shore crabs to small fish.

There are few better seashore picnics than freshly boiled shrimps. Use a large pan of boiling seawater and toss the shrimps in so they are killed outright. Peel and eat them immediately. Fantastic!

Potted Shrimp

Easy! Boil your shrimps and drain them. Push them into a ramekin and force as many as you can into the pot. Melt some butter, add a big pinch of salt and some pepper and fill the pot with hot, seasoned butter. Finish off with a pinch of cayenne pepper.

If you go a little further out and sweep the beach with the water at waist height you are likely to collect Dover sole and sand eel. The eel can be thrown back, but the Dover sole should be killed and eaten, ideally poached with a slice of lemon.

Lobsters and More

Lobster pots are supposed to be controlled. Around the coast there are many who catch lobsters to sell them on the black market. But if you have a few pots (actually called creels and made from string) for personal use no one will bother you. A creel might cost £20 but it will last for a long time. If you beachcomb you can even frequently find them washed up on the shore. However you acquire them, simply sink them with a float and wait for a few days. Our native lobsters are the best in

Precycle!

the world andare around twice the size of those you get from Canada.

Langoustine, also known as Norway lobster, are trawled for, which is a little bit like hoovering the sea, but if you have a boat you can drag a net a couple of hundred yards out and get a bucket full, especially in late Spring.

Taramasalata

This is not the pink stuff we have become so familiar with. The smoked cod's roe can be bought from most fish mongers.

You Will Need:

40g (2oz approx.) sliced white bread
200g (6oz) smoked cod's roe
200ml (⅓ pint) olive oil
2½ tbsps of lemon juice
50ml (1 pint) warm water

Remove the crusts from the bread. (Put them aside, make breadcrumbs and freeze them for when you might need them). Soak the slices for 60 seconds in water and squeeze them until they are almost dry. Skin the roe and break it into chunks. Put the bread and roe in a bowl and use a hand-held mixer or a wooden spoon to mix them. Add the oil gradually as you mix.

Start slowly, building up the speed gradually. When most of the oil has been added, add the lemon juice, then the water, little by little to create a smooth and creamy mix. If it's too stiff, just add more water.

Dairy Products

Butter, Cream and All Things Dairy

Making butter is a very easy process and is also great fun. There are so many different butters in the shops, ranging from spreadable and flavoured to blended and natural that the cost of butter is now as much a factor of added value as anything else. It is possible, for a comparable cost or less and if you shop wisely ie. reduced, to buy cream and make butter at home. And then you can add to it and make soft blends too. Or you can make olive oil butter that is better for you.

The way butter has been made for centuries is by using a butter churn which is a lidded container with a handle in the lid. The cream is placed in the container and the lid fitted tightly. The handle is then turned and the cream churned which means that the fat separates from the liquid and butter is the result.

In the past butter churns have been made out of wood and glass, but they are often made out of metal or plastic these days. Our method doesn't use a churn at all, but relies on a plastic milk bottle.

Precycle!

A 500ml carton of double cream and an empty two litre plastic bottle is all you need to make your butter. Pour the carton of cream into the bottle, put the lid back on, making sure that it is secure and shake it up and down as fast and as vigorously as you can. It is good exercise. Keep the shaking going till you hear the cream separate. This sounds rather like a heavy thud in the bottle accompanied by the splashing sound of the separated liquid.

If all you get is whipped cream, then persevere. You are smply not there yet! You could put a sterilised marble or pebble in the mix. Further shaking will now quickly turn the whipped cream to butter.

Remove the lid and pour the liquid into a jug. This is buttermilk and can be used in other recipes, such as making scones. It is also very popular with most pets. Now cut round the widest part of the bottle and scoop out the solid mass that remains.

Put this into a colander and rinse it under a slow stream of cold water, chopping into the butter to get rid of the rest of the buttermilk. The more you can get rid of, the better the butter tastes and also it will keep longer; it is the buttermilk which eventually turns rancid Keep the running water to a trickle and MAKE SURE IT IS COLD! otherwise your butter will all wash away!

The first salting brings out the rest of the buttermilk from the butter and, once this is done, rinse the butter and taste it for saltiness. Add a little salt to taste if required and put it onto a cold plate or a chopping board.

You can soften your butter by adding a teaspoon of olive or sunflower oil to give both flavour and spreadability. We store the butter in ramekins and a teaspoon of oil per ramekin is usually more than adequate.

The quality of the butter is of course dependent on the quality of the cream. You can improve this further by adding a little crème fraiche to the cream before it is churned. You could also leave the cream to increase in acidity for a day or so before churning it.

Of course, once you've made butter you can not only spread it on bread but you can adapt it to make all sorts of flavoured butters.

Sage Butter

You Will Need:

12 fresh sage leaves
100g (3½ oz) butter, softened
4 tsps wholegrain mustard
salt and freshly ground black pepper to taste

Cream all the ingredients together, chill them in the fridge and use as a filling for pork or chicken fillets/kievs.

Almond Butter

You Will Need:

½ cup of softened butter
1 tbsp of finely chopped almonds
½ tsp almond extract

Mix all the ingredients together. Use this almond butter with quick breads, muffins, pancakes, and other breads.

Brandy Butter

You Will Need:

100g (3½ oz) butter
30g (1oz) soft brown sugar
4 tbsps brandy

Cream the butter and sugar together till fluffy, then add the brandy gradually.

Yogurt

Some yogurts are full of agents to keep them from going off on the shelf so, in order to make the very best, you need to do it yourself.

Making your own yogurt is a simple enough process that will give you a large number of options in the kitchen. It is completely easy and trouble free, and you can make it for no more than the cost of the milk which, if you have your own, is negligible. But this is about more than saving money.

Yogurt can be used to make bread, on breakfast cereals, as an ingredient in curries and stews of all kinds, as a treatment for digestive disorders, for mild skin irritations, as a face mask or a shampoo and can be used to make cheese. It is an absolute must in the home.

All you are doing is starting the cheese making process with specific bacteria and you can get these from the supermarket in live yogurt. You can also buy freeze dried bacterial cultures from specialist suppliers, usually those supplying the smallholder community.

You can, of course, save a little of your yogurt to inoculate your next batch of milk, but I would be careful not to do it too often. When you are growing microbes you have to be sure you are only growing the good ones. If you continue to reuse your batch time and again, then eventually you will get something in there you don't want. So make it a rule not to reuse inoculated milk more than twice, and then to buy some fresh.

You Will Need:

1 litre (2.2 pints) of milk
a couple of tbsps live natural unflavoured yougurt

Sterilise your milk because it will probably contain all kinds of bacteria and we want to have a totally blank canvass on which to work. Do not be tempted to use unsterilised milk. Even pasteurised milk is not good enough for this process. Please do not fall into the trap of thinking that completely untreated milk is better for you. There might be a case for saying so if you know the animal your milk comes from and exactly how that animal lives, its health status and the feed on which it has been fed, but only then it's still a 'might.' Most people haven't a clue about the status of the milk they use, so please make sure you make your milk safe before you use it!

Cool your milk and warm your starter. The temperature you are aiming for with the milk is around 30°C and get your starter up to room temperature. Making the starter is easy; just add a couple of tablespoons of live yoghurt to a little milk or empty the packet into a little milk. You can use a sterile thermometer to check the temperatures. If it is too hot you will simply kill the bacteria.

Allow the yoghurt to incubate. This can take a day and is completely temperature dependent. You can buy thermostatically controlled yogurt makers that keep the tem-

Precycle!

perature at 40°C, the optimum for this stage. But you can simply leave the container in a warm room. It will take a little longer, but it will still work. Do make sure, though, that the container is covered.

Stop the incubation process by placing the yogurt in the fridge and cooling it. It is then ready to serve and to use to inoculate a second batch. Of course, you can use all kinds of flavourings or use it in various other dishes.

Cheese from Yogurt

We have already said that in making yogurt you are starting the cheese making process, so it should come as no surprise that you can continue this to get some cheese. All you need to do is to carefully and evenly mix a teaspoon of salt into a litre (2 pints) of yogurt and leave it overnight. Then spoon this mixture into a muslin bag and hang it up so that the liquid (whey) can drain during the whole of a day. You now have a soft cheese that is perfect for dipping. Place it in the fridge before serving.

Cheese

Most people believe it comes in little slabs, either wrapped in plastic, or in tubs. It's smelly or fattening, bad for your heart or skin and eaten by old men with brandy and fat cigars! It's time to dispel a few myths about cheese.

People say they want to be in control of what is in their food, but spend a fortune allowing others to decide for them. If we all made our own there would be no need for an organic movement in the shops; it would be a grassroots thing with ordinary people making ordinary food. If you make your own cheese you know what is in your food, to a certain extent. You would have to buy organic milk to be completely sure that what you have on your cracker does not also contain a whole bunch of antibiotics, pesticides and cow hormones. Or, of course, keep your own milk animal.

The very minimum you need for cheese making is a stockpot, a colander and a muslin. With this you can make cottage cheese and, with a bit of ingenuity, soft and semi-soft cheese. You will need a minimum of a gallon-sized pot. Your next purchase should be a thermometer that you can get from a brewing supplier or one of the smallholding supplies shops. For cheese making, temperature is all important and you will need to be able to control the heat of a gallon of milk within one degree.

It is true that once you acidify milk it will curdle and you can then collect these curds to make a simple country cheese. After a while, however, you will get bored with lemon tasting cheese and you will want to branch out.

The next stage is to farm your bacteria. Starters are a way of inoculating milk with bacteria that gives the cheese certain qualities. You can buy ready made starters, important for all hard cheeses, from cheese making suppliers, or you can make your own too.

Most cheeses need rennet. This is an amazing and almost mystical substance. The first cheeses were probably made using the natural acidity of sour milk, but it wouldn't be long before someone noticed that milk in a calf's stomach was set. An enzyme called rennet is responsible for this, and for a long time it only came from the stomachs of slaughtered calves. However, over a hundred years ago we discovered that lady's bedstraw juice also set milk. Today you can buy rennet that has been manufactured from genetically altered bacteria – just like many pharmaceuticals.

Precycle!

Because rennet is an enzyme, once it has done its bit of chemistry the process releases the molecule to repeat its job on the next bit of milk protein, so you only need a few drops. Read the label of your particular product and follow the quantities to the letter.

Presses

The problem with cheese is getting rid of the whey. This sugar-laden liquid is the stuff that tends to go off. The protein and fat does not go off so quickly. So, to make your cheese last you need to expel as much whey as possible. This is helped considerably by using a cheese press. The curds are ladled into a mould and a 'follower' is placed on top. This is then rammed down by slowly increasing the pressure, forcing the whey out.

You can use weights such as tins of food or bags of potatoes, but eventually you will want to buy a press. There are lots of designs from Dutch ones with pull down handles to Italian ones with big screws on the top. You can get away with using a G-clamp but they don't stand upright and you cannot collect the whey which would disappoint the dog and the cat who like the whey.

When you get this far there are also lots of things to buy too; round knives for pulling plugs of cheese, wax for painting cheeses such as Edam, cheese brushes, shelving for maturing, humidity sensors.The list is endless.

A simple cream cheese

You Will Need:

4.5 litres (1 gallon) of milk
4 drops of rennet
A starter (in this case some plain yogurt or crème fraiche)
salt
a sterile bowl to collect the curds
a sterile knife
several sterile muslin sheets
a sterile stockpot

Put the milk in the pot with a small tub of crème fraiche or some yogurt. (Try it both with and without to find out how the different components alter the flavour of the cheese.) Leave it for 30 minutes. The point of this is to acidify the milk and to add some richness too!

Warm the milk until it is just warm to the touch, or 28°C if you are using a thermometer. Dissolve your rennet into a cup of cooled, boiled water and add it to the milk.

Remove from the heat and leave it to stand for 30 minutes. You will be able to feel that the surface of the milk has set a little like a jelly. If you thrust your finger into the curd it should break into a small crack. This is called a clean break. Cut the curds into cubes a couple of centimetres across and then pour them into a colander lined with cheesecloth (muslin) to drain. Bring the corners of the muslin together and hang the cheese overnight to drain. If you have no visible hooks you might wish to use kitchen cupboard handles as we have sometimes done.

In the morning, open the cheesecloth and incorporate a teaspoon of salt into it. Give it a good mix and taste it to see if it is salty enough.

Precycle!

You can spread this simple cheese on bread, add chives, fruit, onions, garlic or cream and loosely mix it like a creamed cottage cheese. Alternatively you can put it into a press and make a semi-hard cheese. You can use it in recipes for pasta, in a fondu or on a pizza. You can add sugar and less salt and use it in sweets. You can eat it neat on crackers or from your fingers!

If you do press this cheese hard enough you will get a crumbly cheese a little like Lancashire cheese but not cheddar. A hard cheese is made by the action of bacteria that are introduced at the starter stage. It is their action in the ripening cheese that causes it to become hard but, of course, the pressing helps too.

Edam

This is the archetypal Dutch cheese that usually comes waxed. They are sometimes coloured with a cheese dye, but I don't bother with this myself. The texture and consistency comes from the starter and the scalding of the cheese, but not the pressing, which is quite light. This one uses a thermophilic starter, which means the bacteria are able to withstand a higher temperature than normal. Mesophilic starters are not used in cheeses that call for high temperatures. You can buy these starters readily from cheese making suppliers or from smallholder suppliers. When you buy them you should keep them in the fridge and all you need to do is follow carefully the instructions on the packet, which usually means adding it to a little warm milk.

As with all hard cheese making, temperature is the key, so get a good thermometer and stick rigidly to the temperatures in the recipes.

Dairy Products

You Will Need:

4.5 litres (1 gallon) fresh milk
100ml (3fl oz) thermophilic starter culture
4 – 8 drops of rennet (follow the instructions for your particular rennet)
cheesecloth
Some cheese wax, and a brush to apply it

Combine the milk with the starter and increase the temperature slowly to 32°C. Leave it to stand for 30 minutes to cool to room temperature and then add the rennet in a small quantity of cooled, boiled water.

Leave for a further 30 minutes and then cut the curds into 1 cm cubes. Increase the temperature to 38°C while gently stirring the curds every now and again. Once this temperature is reached remove from the heat.

Allow the curds to settle for 40 minutes and then carefully pour off the whey. Wash the curds in boiled water that has been allowed to cool to a little cooler than hand hot.

Line a colander with a cheesecloth and allow the curds to drain for 15 minutes. Sprinkle 1% salt (by weight) over them.

Press the cheese for a day on either side with a light pressure. Authentically the cheese should be brined at this point (though I have enjoyed it as it is; a dreadful thing to do, I know). Brine it in a weak solution (200g salt per litre or 4oz per pint) for two days, turning the cheese over every few hours. Leave it to dry and then wax. Red is the traditional colour, although green is used for herb flavoured varieties and black for spicy. Allow the cheese to stand for a month.

Precycle!

Blue Wensleydale Cheese

This was originally a ewe's milk cheese. It was made by the tenant farmers who lived on the estates owned by the great Abbeys of Yorkshire, which then owned most of Northern England. It is now made from cow's milk and you can get both white and blue types. I have used it here to show the use of Penicillium Roqueforti, which you can buy from any cheese making supplier.

You Will Need:

4.5 litres (1 gallon) of really creamy milk
100ml (3fl oz) mesophilic starter culture
1g (eighth of a tsp) Penicillium Roqueforti
4 drops of rennet in a little cooled, boiled water
salt

Mix the milk, Penicillium Roqueforti and the starter and heat to 30°C. Add the rennet and wait for an hour for it to set.

Cut the curds into 2cm cubes and allow to stand for 30 minutes in that time raising the temperature to 33°C. Then pour into a colanderlined with cheesecloth and drain for 20 minutes. Re-cut the curds into 1 cm cubes and drain off any remaining whey. Salt at 2% by weight.

Put the curds into a lined mould and press lightly overnight. Wrap the cheese in a sterile cheesecloth and ripen it for a month.

After a fortnight of maturing, pierce the cheese with a very hot needle. Where the air gets in the cheese will be blue due to the action of the Penicillium Roqueforti.

The Bakery

Simple Loaves to Tea Loaves

It is a sad reflection on the world that so many people think they need a special electronic bread maker to make their own bread. Of course nothing could be further from the truth and I would like to challenge anyone to a race me with me, a bowl and my hands, and you with your bread machine. I will win every time.

Making your own bread has never been easier, but the thing that puts most people off is probably the difficulties they foresee in using yeast. However, with fast action dried yeast in easy-to-measure sachets readily available, there is no reason to worry about bread making at home. Always remember that yeast needs a warm environment to work, so the key to successful bread making is a warm kitchen and accurately following a few simple rules.

Precycle!

A Simple Loaf

You Will Need:

900g (2lb) strong white flour
2 level tsps salt
1 sachet fast action dried yeast
1 tbsp sunflower or rapeseed oil
450–568ml ($^3/_4$ –1 pint) warm water

The water must be warm but not hot as this will kill the yeast. Dip your finger in and it should feel comfortably warm. The amount of water required depends on the flour. Start with the lesser amount and add more if the dough isn't soft enough. It should be moist and soft, but not sticky as it will then become difficult to knead.

Sieve the flour and salt together in a large bowl and stir in the yeast. Make a well in the centre of the flour and add the water and oil. Mix with a wooden spoon until all the liquid is combined with the flour. Use your hands to finish combining all the ingredients. Check the water content; too little means the dough won't rise enough so the bread will be heavy and too much means it will be difficult to handle at the kneading stage.

Begin kneading in the bowl. Kneading is a very important stage in bread making as it determines the outcome of the finished loaf. The more you knead the dough, the softer and lighter the finished loaf will be. The action of kneading is quite simple: hold the dough steady with one hand and pull at it with the other. Pull at the edge, stretching it away from you, then fold it back over the rest of the dough. Repeat this action constantly for ten minutes. If you find it easier, do the kneading on a floured surface. I usually start in the bowl and finish the task on the worktop.

Shaping the dough is very easy, especially if you are using loaf tins. You will make two 450g (1lb) loaves with the quantities given in this recipe. Oil your tins and keep them warm. Divide the dough into two equal parts and shape into an oval.

Next comes the proofing stage. This allows the yeast to do its job of making the dough rise. If the tins have been kept warm the dough will begin to rise immediately. It needs to double in size and, if kept in a warm place and covered with a clean teacloth, this should take about 35–40 minutes. Check after 25 minutes as it can lose its shape easily if it rises too much.

Once your loaf has risen you can add a finishing touch to the crust. For a shiny finish try egg and milk brushed over the top – this looks especially good if the bread is a gift.

Last comes the baking. This has two main purposes. The first and most obvious one is to make the bread edible and the second is to kill the yeast. Having your oven very hot does the latter as yeast is sensitive to high temperatures. This is done in the first five to six minutes of cooking, so some recipes ask for the temperature to be turned down slightly so as not to burn the bread. This is especially necessary if your bread is large as you will find it may still be raw in the centre if the heat is too high. Two loaves of the size in our recipe should be baked for 25–30 minutes at 220°C (430°F Gas mark 7). To check if the loaf is cooked thoroughly, lift it out of the tin using oven gloves and tap the bottom of the loaf. It should produce a thudding sound. If not it requires five minutes extra cooking time.

Once cooked you must let it cool. This is very important as the loaf is very difficult to slice when hot and will easily lose its shape, so let it cool completely before eating. Take the loaves out of the tins as soon as they are removed from the oven and place them on a cooling tray. If you leave them in the tin, the crust may become soggy from the moisture which accumulates around the bread in the tin.

Once you have mastered baking a simple loaf a whole world of different recipes is open to you. This above recipe is also great for making small individual rolls, the number dependent on the size of dough you use for each one. You could make a large round cob too and lots of smaller ones.

Naan

Naan is a fantastically flavoursome bread and is easy to make. It has to be cooked very quickly which gives it a hard crust and, at the same time, a soft, stretchy inside.

You Will Need:

225g (8oz) strong white flour
½ tsp salt
1 sachet yeast
4 tbsps warm milk
1 tbsp sunflower oil
2 tbsps plain yogurt
1 egg, beaten

Mix together the flour, salt and yeast in a bowl. Add the milk, oil, yogurt and the beaten egg. Knead for 10 minutes and leave to prove for 30 minutes. Towards the end of the proving time, heat an oiled baking sheet at 230°C Gas mark 8.

Divide into 3 sections and roll out each into the traditional teardrop shape. Place on the hot baking sheet and put in the hottest part of your oven for 3-4 minutes.

Chapattis

You can actually make chapattis by using any kind of flour. I have used both strong, self-raising and plain at times and you get a great result every time, adding water and perhaps just a pinch of salt. That is all you do, then simply mix, roll and flatten. I love watching people make these communally, rolling them out with a stick. This recipe will also work well for tortillas.

Chapattis are traditionally cooked on a tava, a cast iron plate, using atta flour. But they are easily made using a large heavy-based frying pan or a griddle and cooked lightly on both sides. If you cannot find atta flour then wholemeal is fine. This recipe will make approximately 8 chapattis.

You Will Need:

225g (9oz) wholemeal flour
150-180ml (5-7fl oz) water
½ tsp salt

Place the flour in a bowl and add the water slowly, combining with a wooden spoon. Knead lightly until the dough is pliable. Heat a frying pan over a medium heat.

Divide the dough into 8 pieces, knead into a ball and roll out on a lightly floured surface. Shake off any excess flour and place one in the hot pan. Cook for a minute or so and turn and cook the other side.

You can make poori in a very similar manner to chapattis by just adding 2 tablespoons of sunflower oil and reducing the water by 30ml. Roll them out in the same way as chapattis but cook instead in a little vegetable oil about 1cm deep. If the poori start to float, keep pressing them under the oil until they are light and puffy in texture. Turn the poori over for a few seconds then place on some kitchen paper to get rid of any excess oil. Keep them warm if not serving straight away or they will lose their crispness.

You can make a huge batch, freeze them between sheets of greased paper and use them as required.

Soda Bread

Soda bread needs to be eaten on the same day as it is baked, but this shouldn't be a problem once you have tasted it. The following recipe requires buttermilk, which can either be bought or left over from your butter making.

You Will Need:

450g (1lb) self-raising flour
a level tsp salt
a level tsp baking powder
284ml (9fl oz) carton buttermilk or
280 ml (9fl oz) home made buttermilk

Preheat the oven to 220°C Gas mark 7 and grease a baking tray with a little oil.

Sift the flour, salt and baking powder together in a large mixing bowl. Stir in the buttermilk and bind to a soft dough; the mixture should be a little sticky. Add a little more milk or water if the mixture seems dry. Form into a round and place it on a baking tray, cutting across the top of the loaf to make four sections and bake for 20-25 minutes until golden brown.

Quick Granary Loaf

Wholemeal flour needs a little more liquid than white flour, so you will need to adjust the amounts of liquid, adding about 20ml (an ounce or so) extra if using whole-meal on its own. Granary flour is now widely available and makes for a tasty and filling bread. It also gives a very nutty flavour to the loaf.

You Will Need:

450g (1lb) white strong flour
450g (1lb) granary flour
1 sachet fast action dried yeast
568ml (1 pint) warm water or a little more,
depending on the flour used
1 tbsp sunflower oil
2 level tsps salt

Use exactly the same method as for the previous simple white loaf.

Individual rolls

These will keep better in an airtight container rather than a bread bin. Finish them off with a variety of seeds on top of each roll, using either poppy, onion, sesame or fennel seeds.

You Will Need:

700g (1lb 8oz) strong white or brown flour
2 tsps salt
1 sachet fast action dried yeast
1 tbsp sunflower oil
400ml (¾ pint) warm water

Precycle!

Sieve the salt and flour together in a bowl. Add the yeast and stir well. Pour the water into the centre of the flour and add the oil, mixing well with a wooden spoon and use your hands to combine the mixture into a ball.

Knead for 10 minutes and break the dough into 18 small pieces, shaping them as required Place them on an oiled baking sheet a few centimetres apart and leave to prove for 30 minutes. Then bake for 15-20 minutes at 220C Gas mark 7.

Rye Bread

This is a kind of pumpernickel and you can add nuts and seeds of all kinds to taste.

You Will Need:

300g (10oz) rye flour
200g (6oz) strong white flour
300g (10 oz) oats
3 tsps salt
25g (1 oz) fresh yeast
250ml (half a pint – approx.) warm water
1 tsp sugar

Crumble the fresh yeast into the water and add the sugar. Mix all the dry ingredients together in a large bowl. Add the yeast and sugar mixture and combine with your hands until it forms a ball. Add a little more warm water if the dough feels too stiff. Knead this in a bowl for 5 minutes then transfer to a lightly floured surface and knead for a further 5 minutes.

Put it back in the bowl, cover with a clean tea towel and leave it to prove for 30 minutes.

Knock it back and knead for a few more minutes, shape and place in a lightly oiled 2lb loaf tin to prove for 30 minutes. Bake for 25-35 minutes at 200°C Gas mark 6.

Basic Scones

The following are some, but not all, of the various cakes and sweet breads you can buy from the supermarket. Scones are one of the easiest treats to make and home-made they taste much better than any shop bought ones. It's especially the taste as they just begin to cool and the butter or cream melts temptingly down the sides.

There are many scone recipes and, having made the basic one, you can begin to experiment with any combination of fruit, cheese, cherries and all sorts of scone. Don't forget you can also make scones with buttermilk left over from butter making, or any whey left over from cheese making.

You Will Need:

450g (1lb) self-raising flour
1 level tsp salt
1 tbsp golden caster sugar
55g (2 oz) butter chopped into small pieces
1 tbsp lemon juice
400ml (¾ pint) milk

This recipe uses lemon juice in order to acidify the milk which will sometime make it curdle slightly This makes the scone light as it reacts with the bicarbonate of soda in the baking powder.

Pre-heat the oven to 220°C Gas mark 7. Sift the flour and salt together in a mixing bowl and stir in the sugar. Add the butter and rub lightly into the flour using your fingertips until it looks like fine breadcrumbs. Add the

Precycle!

lemon juice to the milk and stir vigorously. The milk should begin to thicken slightly. Mix this into the flour with a fork using quick, light strokes. This should form a soft, pliable dough.

If it is too sticky the mixture will spread and the scones will be a funny shape, but it must be soft as the dough will rise better to make a lighter scone. Bring the dough together by kneading it lightly.

Press them out lightly onto a floured surface. The dough needs to be about 2.5cm (1in.) thick. Using either a fluted or a plain cookie cutter, press straight down into the dough without twisting the cutter as, if you twist your scone it won't rise as much. Each time you make another shape dip your cutter into a little flour. This will make removing the cutter easier. There is some debate as to whether you should use a rolling pin. Traditionalists say that scones should be lightly pressed and only by hand.

This quantity should make about twelve scones. Place each one on a lightly oiled baking tray, brush the tops with a little milk and bake in the oven for 20 minutes till they are a golden brown in colour.

If you are eating them straight away, allow 10 minutes to cool as they are impossible to slice in half if they are too hot. If required they will keep warm and soft wrapped in a tea-towel for an hour or so. Serve them with cream and a jam of your choice or just with butter.

Farmhouse Malt Loaf

This recipe is for a true malt loaf. We often have this as a dessert with a hot drink after a meal. It is also good served with a strong flavoured cheese such as Stilton or a farmhouse cheddar. This malt loaf also must be left for 2-3 days to allow the flavours to develop and for it to moisten and acquire the traditional sticky texture. It is also easy to overcook it as the colour is dark to begin with and it takes quite a long time to cook. Always check the loaf after about 50 minutes by testing how firm the mixture is. If it has stopped being too springy then it is probably cooked. Times will depend on your oven so do regard both temperatures and cooking times as a guide rather than a strict rule. Your local health food or home brew shop usually sells malt.

You Will Need:

225g (7oz) self-raising flour
225g (7oz) sultanas
50g (2oz) muscovado sugar
170g (5½ oz) malt extract (available from health food or home brew stores)
1 tbsp black treacle
2 eggs
150ml (5fl oz) tea

Sift the flour into a bowl and stir in the fruit. Heat the malt, treacle and sugar gently in a pan, then pour over the flour and stir. Add the beaten eggs and tea and beat the mixture well until smooth and combined.

Pour it into 2 buttered 1lb loaf tins and bake for 1hour in a preheated oven at 150°C Gas mark 2.

Precycle!

Bara Brith

This is a Welsh fruited tea loaf, the name meaning 'speck-led bread'. It is very tasty with just a little butter.

You Will Need:

400g (14oz) self-raising flour
350g (13oz) mixed raisins, currants and sultanas
with added candied peel if you wish
275ml (½ pint) tea
2 tbsps honey
1 egg, beaten
80g (3oz approx.) soft brown sugar
1 tsp mixed spice

Soak the fruit in the tea overnight.

Sift the flour and spice into a large mixing bowl and stir in the sugar. Add the fruit and tea mixture, the egg and honey and stir thoroughly.

Pour the mixture into a buttered 2lb loaf tin and cook for 1½ to 1¾ hours at 170°C Gas mark 3.

Breakfast Cereal

From Porridge to Cereal Bars

Amongst the largest of the fortunes made in the modern world are those of the breakfast giants. Kellogg and Quaker have made their fortunes selling cereals and some of their products are very difficult to simulate in the home, but you can certainly make some very good and nutritious breakfast cereals quite easily.

Homemade Cornflakes

If you really want to be the most dedicated of 'precyclers' then do this. It doesn't always work, but if you have your own corn then you can certainly take a stab at making something that approximates to cornflakes. You need to boil the maize until it is quite soft and then pull off the kernels individually. Roll them flat using a rolling pin. This is hard work and you have to get them as flat as possible. The individual kernels are then spread evenly on a tray and baked until they are quite crisp. A moderate to cool oven will do this. The trick is to get them out before they burn, but they must be dry. Turn them over every 15 minutes or so. You can dust them with sugar on both sides if you wish before the drying process. The moisture on the crushed kernels will enable the sugar to stick.

An average tray will equate to a single large portion so, for most purposes, this process is a waste of your time if you are hoping to save money. Mr. Kellogg has secured the monopoly on smashing up corn. However, it is great fun and, when it works, it does so really well.

Granola

This is a great alternative to cereal bars and cereals in general, and you can make so many different variations. In its basic form it is sweetened oats with the addition of other ingredients such as wheat, nuts, fruit, honey and whatever else is around. You bake the materials and allow it to cool into cakes. With the popularity of various sized silicone rubber baking trays you can now make bars that suit your own personal requirements, breaking them up or cutting as appropriate.

They can be eaten as a bar or from a bowl with milk and sugar and, once you get used to the idea of not eating something like Weetabix, you won't look back.

A Simple Granola Recipe

You Will Need:

1 tbsp sunflower oil
2 tbsps of honey
175g (6oz) rolled oats
1 tbsp each of sesame seeds, sunflower seeds,
chopped nuts and raisins
½ tsp cinnamon

Preheat the oven to 160°C Gas mark 3. Combine the oil and honey and mix with the other ingredients. Spread evenly on a non-stick baking tray and cook for 30 minutes, making sure it doesn't burn.

One of the best things about granola is that you can add almost anything to it. The main constituent is oats and this should be at least 50% of the total weight of the mix. Try adding sesame seeds, wheat kernels, coconut flakes, chopped apple, dates or grapes. There really is no end to the possibilities.

Oats

Samuel Johnson said that oats were a crop grown in England to feed horses and in Scotland to feed people, but it has to be said that oats are in fact nothing less than a miracle food. The Scots have lived off them for many generations and this is something the rest of us should be doing too!

Oats have none of that amazing protein, gluten, which is found in wheat and makes it all elastic and springy. Therefore oats are no good for making what you might call a good loaf. At best it would comes out all cakey. The problem is that the gluten is needed to capture the carbon dioxide and force the bubbles to make the bread light. You can make oat bread but you need some ordinary strong flour to help bind it if using yeast, or you can use ordinary flour if you are making soda bread.

Oats stimulate healthy bowels and are said to help reduce blood cholesterol levels. Eating oats has been shown in a number of double blind tests to cut the risk of both heart disease and strokes. The fact that there is no gluten in oats is a major brnefit for people who are intolerant to it. Whole oats have a low glycaemic index, which is also important for the regulation of blood sugar.

Herbal medicine has long used oats to help with sleeping problems, but it can also serve as a stimulant. Horses

Precycle!

fed too many oats can become excitable, but the same property can actually help people with depression. Oats contain many nutrients, more protein than wheat and more B vitamins.

Porridge

Porridge is easy to make, but it is one of the basics of life that absolutely everyone should be able to make and, since many schools no longer teach cooking, there are millions out there who, through no fault of their own, have never learned! This recipe serves 2.

You Will Need:

500ml (1 pint) of water
(or milk or half milk and water)
50g (2oz) oats
1g (a generous pinch) salt
20g (1oz) sugar
a flavouring of your own (I personally like golden syrup)

Bring the liquid to a gentle simmer. If you are just using milk you need to get it to the bubbling stage, but don't let it boil. Add the oats and stir them in well together with the sugar and salt.

Simmer and then turn the heat right down. Put a lid on your pan and cook like this for about ten minutes. The rougher the oats, the longer it will take.

The flavouring can be added in the serving bowl. Cream, crème fraîche, honey, maple syrup, golden syrup, mint, thyme, jam and lemon are all possibilities. The Swedes, a great porridge eating nation with many names for different textures and types of porridge, add a lingon berry sauce, which is a little like cranberry sauce or cinnamon, adding a little sugar to taste. The range of likes and dislikes with porridge is immense. Some insist it should be made with just water and salt whilst others like all sorts of creamy and sweet additions.

Muesli

Muesli originates from Switzerland and eastern central Europe, mostly in the late Victorian times, but is now eaten all over the world. You can mix your own according to taste and preference. Don't mix huge quantities because it does tend to settle and the action of remixing (i.e. shaking it up in the container) changes the consistency of the oats. As long as oats make up around a third of your total ingredients, you can't go wrong.

You Will Need:

115g (3½ oz) rolled oats
30g (1oz) dried apricots
30g (1oz) dried prunes
30g (1oz) chopped apple
1 tbsp raisins or sultanas
1 tbsp chopped dates
2 tbsps chopped, toasted almonds, hazelnuts or pecans
2 tbsps wheatgerm

It is best prepared the night before with a mixture of 75:25 milk to cream and a little sugar or honey. Put this in the fridge overnight and serve for breakfast! Yummy! I also once knew a vegan vegetarian who placed it in the fridge overnight with just water in place of the milk and insisted it was delicious.

Mixed Seed Honey Crunch

This is good to make for a sticky breakfast that is a bit like granola, but without the thing all sticking together in a lump. You have to toast the seeds and oats on a skillet

Precycle!

or a large, heavy pan. No oil is used as you are simply heating the dry seeds. Try a tablespoon each of sesame seeds, flax seeds and sunflower seeds and some coconut flakes. As they are toasting add a cup full of dry rolled oats and get this all hot too. Then turn off the heat and add 3 tablespoons of honey and stir it well into the hot mixture. When this is completely mixed, allow it to cool. It will form sticky nugget sized pieces that fall apart. It is lovely with a little milk.

Biscuits and Cookies

Shortbreads, Brownies and Other Fancies

Biscuit comes from the French language and means 'to bake twice.' Biscuits these days are not always baked twice, but they do have to make a crisp snap when broken. The easiest of all biscuitsto make is shortbread. You can really get your hands in and work this mixture as it requires a fairly rough handling to bring the ingredients together and, unlike pastry, it is better if you have warm hands.

Shortbread

You Will Need:

120g (4oz) softened butter
100g (3oz) unrefined caster sugar
100g (3oz) self-raising flour
100g (3oz) plain flour

Cream the butter and sugar together until soft and fluffy

Precycle!

and sift in both flours at the same time, stirring in with a wooden spoon. Using your hands combine all the ingredients until they form a ball. Press the mixture into a well buttered baking tray or tin.

Prick well all over with a fork and gently press into the outer edge with the pad of your thumb or finger to flute the edge and bake at 180°C Gas mark 4 for 30-35 minutes until golden brown.

Leave to cool for 20 minutes before removing from the tin to a cooling tray and cut into 12 equal fingers. Sprinkle with a little extra sugar if desired.

As a variation to the basic shortbread press halved glace cherries into the dough just prior to baking.

Crispy Jumbles

You Will Need:

100g (3oz) softened butter
150g (5oz) soft brown sugar
150g (5oz) self-raising flour
50g (1½ oz) crispy rice cereal
1 beaten egg
a 100g (3oz) bar of dark chocolate, chopped
or dark chocolate chips

Cream the butter and sugar and beat in the egg. Then fold in the flour and mix in the cereal and chocolate pieces. Put spoonfuls of the mixture onto a greased baking tray about 5cm apart as they spread. Bake for 10-15 minutes at 180C Gas mark 4.

American brownies are a cross between a cake and a

cookie. They are also very easy to make and varying the ingredients can easily change the finished product. Here are two simple but tasty variations, one for chocolate lovers and the other a vanilla flavoured fruit brownie.

Chocolate and Nut Brownies

You Will Need:

100g (3oz) butter
200g (7oz) soft brown sugar
180g (6oz) self-raising flour
20g (1oz) cocoa powder
1 large beaten egg
50g (1½ oz) chopped pecan nuts

Sift the flour and cocoa into a bowl and melt the butter and sugar together in a pan over a low heat. Add this to the flour and mix in the beaten egg and nuts. Combine well to form a moist dough and press into a well greased, shallow tin. Bake at 180°C Gas mark 4 for 15-20 minutes and leave to cool in the tin for 20-30 minutes before transferring to a cooling tray.

Do not overcook it as it is difficult to tell if it is cooked with the cocoa darkening the mixture. Press on the top of the brownie. It should give a little and remain flat if cooked. This is quite different from a cake which should spring back when cooked.

Precycle!

Boston Brownies

You Will Need:

100g (3oz) butter
200g (7oz) unrefined sugar
200g (7oz) self-raising flour
1 large beaten egg
1/3 tsp vanilla extract
50g (½ oz) raisins

Make as above, but add the vanilla after you have mixed in the butter/sugar combination and add the raisins, mixing in well. Another variation is to add cinnamon and chopped apple instead of the vanilla and raisins.

Oat cookies

You Will Need:

120g (4oz) butter
120g (4oz) soft brown sugar
3 tbsps of syrup
160g (5oz) self-raising flour
160g (5oz) porridge oats

Heat the butter, syrup and sugar in a pan until butter has melted and pour in the oats and sift in the flour, mixing well.

Roll the dough to form small balls about the size of a ping pong ball. Place on a greased baking tray about 6cm apart. Gently press ball down and bake at 180C/ Gas 4 for 10-15 minutes. Place on a cooling tray and allow to cool, if you can stop yourself from eating one!
To vary them add 25-30g (1 oz) of chopped almonds after you have added the flour and oats.

Melting Moments

You Will Need:

100g (3oz) softened butter
80g (2oz) unrefined sugar
1 medium beaten egg
4-5 drops vanilla extract
160g (6oz) self-raising flour
2-3 tbsps rolled oats for coating
Glace cherries for decoration

Cream the butter and sugar until light and fluffy and beat in the egg and vanilla. Fold in the flour and mix using your hands to bring it all together. Roll into small balls and coat each one in the oats before placing it on a greased baking tray 4cm (2in) apart.

Place half a glace cherry in the centre of each ball, pressing down lightly to flatten the cookie, then bake for 10-15 minutes at 190°C Gas mark 5.

The final recipe calls for a little more effort, These will need to be rolled out and cut with a round fluted cutter. I prefer the recipes that call for the mixture to be rolled into balls because you never have any left over, whereas when rolling and cutting is involved I always seem to be left with a bit that ends up as a mis-shapen wonder that I have to eat! But these are so delicious and versatile I just feel compelled to make them.

I usually make a large batch, adding raisins to half the mixture and leaving the rest plain. They are deliciously crispy and you will find it virtually impossible to eat just one.

Precycle!

Shrewsbury Biscuits

You Will Need:

130g (3oz approx.) softened butter
160g (5oz) caster sugar
2 egg yolks
220g (7oz) plain flour
the grated rind of 1 lemon

Cream the butter and sugar until fluffy and add the egg yolks, beating well. Then mix in the flour and add the lemon rind. Use your hands to combine and form a ball.

Roll it out on a clean, floured surface to about ½cm deep and, using a cutter, cut out discs of dough and place them on a greased baking sheet.

Bake for 10-15minutes at180°C Gas mark 4 and place on a cooling tray as soon as the biscuits have cooled slightly. They will crisp up as soon as they are cool and can also be topped with a little glace icing or some melted chocolate.

Cakes and Puddings

Basic Cakes to Fancy Puddings

The Victoria sandwich cake is probably the single most traditional and popular of cakes to bake. You can use any flavour of jam to sandwich your cake together. Raspberry is traditional choice but you can use lemon curd or marmalade instead of jam. I have used caster sugar, granulated and soft light brown sugars and have ound the latter makes the lightest and best flavour cake. But don't worry about using whatever sugar you have in as it will always taste delicious if you have made it yourself!

The cake mixture in these recipes is based roughly on equal amounts of fat, sugar, flour, eggs and a little milk if necessary.

If you have never baked a cake before this recipe is so easy to do. Make life easy for yourself and have all the ingredients weighed out ready to use and prepare your tins before you start. The secret of success with this cake is to cream the mixture thoroughly to get as much air as possible into the cake. Sift the flour into the creamed mixture and keep as much air in as possible by carefully folding in the flour and milk. Folding in requires a metal spoon that will cut into the mixture and keep in the air as you combine the flour into the creamed mixture. The following recipe makes 10 large slices and is based roughly on equal amounts of fat, sugar, flour, eggs and a little milk, if necessary.

Precycle!

Victoria Sandwich

You Will Need:

200g (6½ oz) butter, softened to room temperature
200g (6½ oz) soft, light brown sugar
200g (6½ oz) self-raising flour
3 eggs, beaten
2-3 tbsps milk
4 tbsps jam
Caster sugar for dusting over the cake

Grease and line two sandwich tins with silicone paper. Preheat the oven to 170°C Gas mark 3 and cream the butter and sugar together in a mixing bowl until light and fluffy, adding the beaten egg gradually and beating in each lot vigorously. The creaming can be done either with a wooden or plastic spoon or with a hand mixer. If the mixture seems to be curdling or separating, add a tablespoon of the flour along with the egg and this will stop it. Gradually sift the flour into the creamed mixture, folding it in with a metal tablespoon.

The mixture should drop readily off the spoon if moist enough. If not, simply add 2 or 3 tablespoons of milk and stir it in carefully, again with a metal spoon. Put equal amounts of this mixture into the two prepared tins, smoothing out the tops and making a well in the centre to allow the cakes to rise uniformly.

Place the tins in the centre of the oven and leave to cook for 18-20 minutes. Use a timer if, like me, you tend to forget what time the cakes went into the oven.

When cooked the cake should spring back when lightly touched with your finger and should be golden brown in colour. Leave it to cool in the tins for 15 minutes before removing and carefully peeling away the paper.

When completely cool spread the jam over one half and sandwich the two together. Then dust with a little caster sugar to serve.

Iced Cup Cakes

You Will Need:

150g (5oz) butter
150g (5oz) soft, light brown sugar
150g (5oz) self-raising flour
2 eggs, beaten
1-2 tbsps milk

For the icing:
6 rounded tbsps icing sugar
water to mix to a thick but spreadable coating
glace cherries, chocolate buttons, or hundreds and thousands to decorate.

This recipe will make 12 muffin sized cakes. Begin by preheating the oven to 150°C Gas mark 2 and place some paper bun cases in a bun tin into the oven. Then follow stages 2-6 of the Victoria Sandwich recipe and put a dessert spoon of the mixture into each paper case or a teaspoon in the case of smaller cases.
o

Turn the oven up to 170°C Ga mark 3 and bake for 10-15 minutes until golden brown and, whilst cooling, make the icing by sieving the icing sugar into a small bowl and adding 2-3 teaspoons of water. Mix well and add a little more water if necessary to make a thick but runny icing. Spread the icing over the cakes, allowing the icing to coat the top of each cake and decorate with whatever you prefer. I adore glace cherries but you can have fun with all kinds of toppings.

Precycle!

Butterfly Buns

Make these in the same way as the Iced Cup Cakes and leave them to cool completely.

For the Filling You Will Need:

80g (3oz) butter
6 heaped tbsps icing sugar
½ tsp vanilla extract
icing sugar for dusting

Cream the butter in a mixing bowl until soft and fluffy and sift the icing sugar into the butter, beating thoroughly. Add the vanilla extract and mix in well.

Cut a circle out of the top of each cake and place a good dessert spoonful of butter cream into the well. Cut the sponge circle in half and place each half in the top of the butter cream to look like butterfly wings Finish the cakes by dusting them with a little icing sugar.

Pineapple Upside Down Cake

This can be eaten as a dessert with either cream or custard, or sliced and eaten with a cup of tea or coffee. I prefer to use a small can of sliced pineapple in juice as you need the juice to lace the sponge before and after it is cooked.

You Will Need:

150g (5oz) butter
150g (5oz) golden caster sugar
150g (5oz) self-raising flour
2 eggs, beaten
1 small can of pineapples in their own juice
6 glace cherries

Preheat the oven to 170°C Gas mark 3 and grease and line a square 20cm (8in.) cake tin. Place four slices of pineapple in the bottom of the tin and put a cherry in the centre of each slice and in the middle of the four slices.

Follow the Victoria sandwich recipe, replacing the milk with pineapple juice. Then place the cake mixture carefully over the pineapple and cherries and smooth out the top.

Bake for 25 minutes until springy to the touch and golden brown in colour. Just after removing from the oven, skewer the top and drizzle 3-4 tablespoons of pineapple juice over the cake.

Leave it to cool down completely before removing from the tin and turn upside down onto a serving plate. Peel away the silicone paper carefully, taking care not to disturb the pineapple and cherries.

Easy Simnel Fruit Cake

You Will Need:

1 cup soft brown sugar
1 cup mixed dried fruit
1 cup milk
2 cups self-raising flour
120g (4oz) butter
1 tbsp honey
1 level tsp mixed spice
2 eggs, beaten

Preheat the oven to 150°C Gas mark 2 and grease and line a 20cm (8in.) round cake tin. Place the fruit, sugar, butter, honey and spice in a pan on a medium heat. Bring to a gentle simmer and continue to simmer for 5 minutes. Take off the heat and allow to cool completely before sieving in half of the flour and beating in the eggs. Add the rest of the flour and fold into the cake mixture until fully combined.

Place in the cake tin and smooth out the top, making a well in the centre to allow for the cake rising. Bake for 40 minutes at 150°C Gas mark 2, then turn the oven down to150°C Gas mark 1 for a further 40 minutes, or until firm to the touch and a dark, golden brown in colour. Test the centre of the cake with a skewer or a thin knife. If the cake is cooked throughout there should be no cake mixture on the blade when removed. If the cake requires further cooking time, cover it with foil and leave to cook for a further 10-15 minutes.

Leave in the tin to cool for 30-40 minutes, then remove from the tin and peel away the paper. Leave to cool completely before wrapping in greaseproof paper and placing in an airtight container. Allow the flavour and moistness to develop for 1-2 days before eating.

Baked Vanilla Cheesecake

You Will Need:

For the base:
300g (9½oz) digestive biscuits, crushed
100g (3oz) unsalted butter, melted

Combine the two ingredients and press into a greased 20cm (8in.) spring form tin. Place it in the fridge to firm up.

You Will Need:

For the the filling:
600g (1lb 3oz) cream cheese
200g (6oz) very thick cream
230g (7oz) icing sugar

2 eggs
½ tsp vanilla extract

Preheat the oven to 150°C Gas mark 2. Beat the cheese, cream and sugar together until light and smooth and add the eggs, one at a time, beating them into the cheese mixture. Beat in the vanilla and place the mixture over the base. Smooth out the top and bake for 1 hour and 10 minutes. Turn the oven off and leave the cake to cool in the oven. This will stop the top from cracking. When cool, remove the sides of the tin, but serve the cheesecake on the tin base on a plate. This prevents having to mess about trying to remove the base and makes it easier to serve.

This cheesecake can be served alone as it is so delicious or can be served with a little fresh cream and any fresh fruit in season. Stew 4-5 tablespoons of fresh blackcurrants with a tablespoon of sugar or honey until just soft, leave to cool and pour over the cheesecake. Strawberries, raspberries or apricots also make a wonderful topping for your cheesecake.

To make the chocolate version melt a 100g (3oz) pack of dark chocolate in a bowl over a pan of hot water and add it to the mixture after you have beaten in the eggs. Make sure the chocolate is thoroughly mixed in and not streaky. Finish the cake in the same way as above.

Precycle!

Ice Cream

Unless you buy the expensive stuff ice cream is actually creamy guar gum mix. Homemade ice cream is cheaper, healthier and more flavoursome. Of course no one can make cheap slurry cheaper than the factories that pump it out but I am taking it as read that you don't really want to make that kind of stuff.

There are two basic ways of making ice cream; one with cream, the other with custard. In effect, as you cool the liquid, the ice crystals form and stick together, making bigger crystals. What you need to do is to slowly freeze the liquid and stir all the time so that the crystals are continuously broken up and remain small. In this way the ice cream, or sorbet, (which is basically ice cream without any cream) freezes as a smooth paste.

Pour your freshly prepared mixture into a fairly wide bowl and put it in your refrigerator to chill for between 1 and 2 hours. How long this takes will depend upon whether you've actually heated up or cooked any of the ingredients when making the mixture. Then remove from the refrigerator and put into your freezer for 30-40 minutes.

Take the bowl out and check the state of the mixture. It should have started freezing from the outside edges in, but should not be fully frozen in the centre of the bowl.

Beat the mixture hard to produce a cream then return it to the freezer for a further 30 minutes. Repeat this several times until you are happy with the consistency of the mixture, then leave in the freezer.

Easy Vanilla Ice Cream

You Will Need:

250ml (½ pint) single cream
1-2 tsps vanilla extract
Small can of condensed milk

You can replace the condensed milk with yoghurt if you like, or simply 50ml (2oz) cream with 2 tablespoons of sugar added. Combine everything and then freeze as above.

From this base you can be really inventive and add all sorts of flavourings to your mixture. For instance, add a few drops or rose flavoured water or orange water.

How to Make Ice

Well you do need ice to make ice and it is actually a simple procedure. In some antique shops you can find old Italian ice cream makers that use this principle. The action of dissolving salt in ice is endothermic; it takes a lot of energy out of the surroundings. If you add salt to ice, the ice melts, but the temperature drops, not increases. So, if you collect a bucket of snow and sprinkle salt into it, a pan of water placed on top will actually freeze. You can use this principle to make ice cream but I tend to use the freezer, if only for the sake of convenience. 'Precycling' doesn't have to be hard work!

Precycle!

Easy Chocolate Sauce

This is ideal for serving hot or cold with ice cream.

You Will Need:

100g (3½ oz) dark chocolate with at least 70% cocoa solids
1 tbsp golden syrup

Melt the chocolate gently in either a double boiler or in a bowl that fits snugly in a pan containing boiling water. When it is fully melted remove it from the heat and stir in the syrup until fully combined.

Rich Chocolate Sauce

This can be served with any dessert, from fresh pears to cheesecake and, it goes without saying, ice-cream.

You Will Need:

150g (5oz) dark chocolate, broken into small pieces
½ a 375ml (⅔ pint approx.) can condensed milk

Heat the condensed milk in a double boiler until hot but not bubbling. Remove it from the heat before the next step. Add the chocolate and stir gently into the condensed milk. This is best served straight away.

Caramel Sauce

You Will Need:

50g (2oz) unsalted butter
50g (2oz) oft brown sugar
375ml (⅔ pint) can condensed milk
1 dessertspoon golden syrup

Put all the ingredients into a pan and heat slowly, stirring to make sure all the sugar is dissolved. Bring to the boil, stirring constantly. Reduce the heat and simmer the sauce until creamy and a fudge colour. Leave to cool before serving. This will keep for a week in a sealed jar, but don't keep this one in the fridge as it will stiffen up too much.

Fruit Sauces

There are 3 basic methods of preparing fruit syrups. Firstly there is preservable syrup which can be stored for 6-8 weeks as long as it is put in sterilised bottles or jars and sealed well. Then there is the hot method. Here the syrup isn't boiled for as long as in the previous recipe and will not keep as long, although it will keep in the fridge for 6-7 days in a sealed container. Finally there are the cold syrups. These sauces need to be used up on the day of their preparation.

Preservable Syrup

You Will Need:

1kg (2.2lb) good quality ripe strawberries
or raspberries, hulled
4 tbsps water
370g (12oz) white caster sugar

Wash the fruit thoroughly and place it in a large pan. If using strawberries cut each fruit in half and add the water. Bring slowly to the boil and cook at boiling point for 3 minutes. Remove from the heat and mash the fruit well, replacing it on a medium heat and simmering until the fruit is tender. This should take about 5 minutes. Allow it to cool. Rub the fruit through a sieve, catching all the juices in another pan.

Add the sugar and heat the syrup over a medium heat

Precycle!

until all the sugar has dissolved. Bring the syrup to the boil and, as soon as the boiling point has been reached, remove from the heat and allow to cool a little. Using sterilised equipment, pour the syrup (using a funnel if it is easier) into bottles or jars. Seal well and store in a cool dark place. Once opened store in the fridge and use within seven days.

Quick Hot Method

Follow the method for preservable syrup but mash the fruit whilst bringing to the boil. Add the sugar and dissolve slowly over a low heat. Once completely dissolved, turn off the heat and serve or store in the fridge when cool.

If you want to make a blackcurrant or a blackberry sauce, add 250ml of water at the cooking stage.

Cold Syrups

You Will Need:

454g (1lb) fruit
4 tbsps icing sugar

Wash the fruit thoroughly and mash it to a puree using either a food processor or a potato masher. If you don't like the seeds you can rub it through a sieve before sieving the icing into the pureed fruit. Stir it well until all the sugar has dissolved and serve.

If you prefer a tangier sauce simply use less sugar and similarly, if you like it sweeter, add a little more sugar.

Teas
and
Cordials

Refreshing Teas and Invigorating Juices

It is actually rather difficult to make your own tea and coffee. They are so distinctive and also such an everyday part of living that there seems to be little way of avoiding buying them. You could buy tea bushes, and the care required is almost exactly the same as for a clematis. However, don't try to make tea from clematis leaves. The tea bush is a type of clematis and you pick the leaves, but not too many, and leave them in the open air, away from the rain, to cure.

Herbal teas are a different matter, though. You will need a good, fine tea strainer, preferably an infuser if you wish to make a single cup, but a small teapot is easy to use. Just place the required amount of herbs or fruit in the strainer or in the pot and leave it to infuse for 5-10 minutes. This is the general rule for all the recipes in this section and where there is any variation it will be made clear in the recipe.

Precycle!

Probably the easiest and most popular herbal tea is peppermint, so we shall begin with this. All weights are approximate in this section because, to be honest, you simply get your herbs and plonk boiling water on them. If you want a stronger brew, add more herbs and for a weaker one add less. It seems a shame to add sugar to such a natural brew. Honey is preferable because the body doesn't have to do anything to the sugars in order to make use of them. Sucrose, as in ordinary sugar, is a complex molecule and therefore has to be broken down before it can be used, but the fructose and glucose in honey are directly useable in the metabolism and are good for diabetics too. If you need to add sugar remember that it is sweeter than honey, so use only about 50% of the quantity.

If you are on medication or pregnant, always seek medical advice before drinking lots of herbal tea.

Peppermint Tea

You Will Need:

1 tsp dried or 1 heaped tsp finely chopped fresh mint leaves
100ml (1 cup) boiling water
This makes one cup of tea but for larger quantities use:
20g (⅔ oz) dried or 30g (1 oz approx.) fresh mint leaves
500ml (1 pint approx.) boiling water
add a little honey if desired.

This will make a small teapot of peppermint tea; ideal for sharing.

Lemon Balm Tea

Lemon balm has traditionally been used as a health tonic. It benefits the general well being of the drinker. John Evelyn (1620-1706) wrote that 'Balm is sovereign for the brain, strengthening the memory and powerfully chasing away melancholy.' Who could argue with this and the mild lemony flavour makes it a very refreshing drink too.

You Will Need:

8g (⅓ oz) finely chopped lemon balm leaves
100ml (1 cup) boiling water
add a little honey to taste if sweetness is required

The next brew is one of my favourites, especially after a very busy day when, even though I am tired, restlessness can prevent relaxation. Chamomile and lavender are both renowned for their calming effects and make a very comforting tea drink in the evening or any time you want a relaxing moment.

Chamomile and Lavender Tea

You Will Need:

1 tsp dried or 1 heaped tsp fresh chopped chamomile flowers
1 tsp dried or 1 heaped tsp fresh lavender flowers (rub the florets off the main stem and they come away easily)
100ml (a cupful) boiling water
Honey to taste

Combine all the ingredients and allow to infuse. Sieve before drinking.

Precycle!

Raspberry and Peppermint Tea

Raspberry leaf tea is traditionally used to prepare women for childbirth, but it also makes a good tea, especially when combined with mint, the addition of dried raspberry fruit adding to the depth of flavour. This tea is excellent to give when ayone has an upset tummy or needs a boost to their appetite.

You Will Need:

1 tsp dried or 1 heaped tsp fresh finely chopped raspberry leaves
1 tsp dried or 1 heaped tsp fresh chopped mint leaves
1 heaped tsp dried, chopped raspberries
100ml (a cupful) boiling water
honey to taste

Mix all the ingredients and leave to infuse for 15 minutes. Sieve before drinking.

Lemon, Honey and Thyme Drink

Lemon is often associated with cold cures and the next recipe is ideal for those times when you feel in less than tiptop condition. The tea is especially good for soothing a sore throat during a cold but it can also be drunk whenever you need a refreshing pick me up.

Contrary to popular belief, lemon is not overflowing with vitamin C. You can make rosehip water that brims with the vitamin and this is done by collecting rosehips and breaking them so that you can see the seeds. Pour a liberal amount of boiling water over them and leave it to go cold. Sieve all the bits out with a muslin and then use this water to make up the recipes. This contains a lot more Vitamin C than lemon juice butit doesn't taste half as good.

You Will Need:

the juice of 1 lemon
1 tsp grated lemon peel (be careful to get only the zest, not
the pith, as this is very bitter)
1-2 tbsps of honey
1 level tsp dried or 1 heaped tsp fresh thyme leaves
100ml (a cupful) boiling water

Put the thyme, juice and peel of the lemon in a jug. Pour over the boiling water and stir well. Sieve into a cup or mug and add honey to taste. This really needs to be sweeter than the other recipes due to it being a cold soother. Drink it comfortably hot.

Sweet Cherry and Cranberry Drink

You can find out how to dry fruit later in the book under the growing section. This drink can be had any time, but is best served cold. Iin the Summer it can be served with ice and the odd fresh cherry.

You Will Need:

12g (½ oz) dried cherries
12g (½ oz) dried cranberries
100ml (a cupful) boiling water
3 or 4 borage leaves
honey to taste

Put the fruit in a teapot or jug. and pour over the boiling water. Add honey and the borage leaves, stirring well and leave to cool down. Sieve if necessary.

Precycle!

Elderflower and Rosehip Tea

You Will Need:

one elderflower umbel
1 crushed rosehip
1 dessert spoon of honey

Normally rosehips are not on the plant at the same time as elderflowers but it really is worth collecting them because they are nature's highest single concentration of vitamin C. They will freeze quite easily and to make this tea all you need to do is defrost one, hitting it with a spoon or a pestle a few times to crack it open a little. Simply put a piece of elderflower umbel into a teapot with the rosehip and pour on some boiling water. Then add the honey and stir. If you need additional flavour, a slice of lemon will suffice.

If you don't have any rosehips replace them with a dessert spoon of rosehip syrup which is still readily available from chemists.

Spicy Lemon Tea

Ginger is a wonderfully warming spice that goes well with the flavour of lemon. It's a great drink for expecting mothers who may feel nausea in the early months of pregnancy, but only take it as described.

You Will Need:

the juice and zest of a lemon
4g (½ tsp) grated fresh ginger
3 tsps honey
100ml boiling water

Mix the ginger, lemon zest and honey together and pour over the lemon juice and boiling water. Stir well and leave for 5 minutes to allow the flavours to develop before consuming. Sieve if required.

Orange and Rosemary Tea

Rosemary has quite a pungent flavour but it goes well with orange and a little cinnamon. It looks great in a long glass with both a slice of orange and some borage flowers.

You Will Need:

the juice of 2 oranges
1tsp dried or 1 heaped tsp fresh rosemary
¼ tsp cinnamon
2 tsps demerara sugar
100ml (a cupful) boiling water

Mix the rosemary, sugar and cinnamon together in a jug and pour over the orange juice. Stir and leave for 10 minutes, then add the boiling water and serve either hot or cold.

Precycle!

Apple Juice

There are so many people who will never realise the sheer bliss of real, homemade apple juice. It's nothing like the watery stuff you can buy in the shops and is so full of chemicals that are good for you, many of which are sadly deactivated in the shop bought product.

Phytochemical is the latest buzzword amongst scientists. These are a series of chemicals that plants use as part of their immune system, but which can also be used by our own immune systems too. It's obvious really. We have always used plant immune systems to augment our own. There are more than 1000 known phytochemicals such as lycopene in tomatoes, isoflavones in soya and flavanoids in fruits. Apples are a rich source of phytochemicals and studies have shown that the consumption of apples reduces the risk of some cancers, cardiovascular disease, asthma and diabetes. In the laboratory apple juice has also been shown to exhibit very strong antioxidant activity which can inhibit cancer cell growth and division, decrease fatty oxidation and lower cholesterol.

To make apple juice you don't really need much equipment. The most important single requirement is a food processor, without which it is very difficult to break the apples up sufficiently to extract the juice.

You can buy presses, but a press will probably not be strong enough to break up the apple on its own and force the juice out. The apple must be chopped up first.

The necessary steps to successful apple juice production are simple enough:

Cut the apples into pieces. Don't worry about the pips or the stalks. Feed them into the food processor and then blast away until the apples are no more than small chips.

There is a lot of juice waiting to come out and you will need to fill your press carefully if you are not to lose a lot of it.

Fill the basket of your press. Large presses for fruit that are made from wooden slats need to have the apple chips wrapped in muslin or else you will lose material out of the sides. When you turn the key on the plunger the apple juice is forced out. You can filter this through muslin if you like, but I prefer to have my juice unfiltered. I do, however, pour it through a tea strainer to remove any larger pieces of fruit.

The process is then repeated until you have used up all your apples. The juice will freeze and lasts a long time. I add a little lemon juice, just a tablespoon per litre (a tsp per pint), which stabilises the liquid and enhances the flavour even more.

You can treat pears in exactly the same way as apples but the juice doesn't last as long. Pears are full of wooden cells called sclerids, which is why they are often used as facial scrubs. You certainly will need to filter pear juice through muslin and must freeze it if you are to keep it for any length of time.

Soft fruit must be washed and wrapped in muslin before pressing, but it frequently mushes to excess and the yield is consequently often low. You are much better making raspberry and strawberry juice by simply boiling the fruit first and then pressing out the juice.

Precycle!

Syrup Drinks

A wonderful way to use up a glut of soft fruit or fruit which has been reduced in price in the supermarket is to make a syrup. This can then be used to make thirst quenching drinks by adding sparkling water, by making milk shakes or by adding it to white wine to make spritzers.

Syrups also make delicious ice-cream sauces. They are very easy to make and require only a few ingredients. The syrup freezes well and can be kept successfully for up to three months. Do make sure you de-frost any syrups thoroughly before use.

The secret is to keep the heating of the fruit to a minimum to retain the full fruit flavour. Fully ripened fruit should produce more than enough juice, but by using a pectin-destroying enzyme you can improve the yield. Use ½ a level teaspoon of enzyme to 220g (8oz) fruit or asper the instructions on the pack.

The only other ingredients you will need are sugar and water. You can use ordinary granulated sugar, but I find caster sugar dissolves easier.

Raspberries and strawberries don't need any water adding to them because they are already full of liquid. Blackcurrants will need 250ml (8oz approx.) for every 500g (1lb approx.) of fruit. Blackberries need less, just 50ml for every 500g of fruit (or 2oz for every pound).

Wash the fruit and remove the stalks or any other similar material. Place it in a heatproof bowl, crush the fruit well with a fork or a potato masher and add the water where necessary. Place the bowl over a pan of boiling water and heat the fruit gently until the juice begins to run. A clean cheesecloth or muslin will be ideal to strain the juice into another bowl or pan, at which point you can add the sugar.

Approximately 250g sugar for every 500ml (or 9oz per pound) of juice will be about right, although taste will determine you own ratios. If you strain the juice into a pan with measurements up the side this will makes it easier. If the sugar doesn't dissolve well you can also use the pan to heat the juice gently over a low light, stirring slowly. Pour the cooled syrup into sterilised bottles using a funnel. It will keep for up to 6 weeks if stored in the fridge.

Lemonade

There is nothing more refreshing than a glass of old fashioned lemonade on a hot summer afternoon! This recipe will also boil down to make a sorbet. Refer to the section on ice cream and follow the instructions as per ice cream.

You Will Need:

4 unwaxed large lemons or 6 smaller ones
400-450g (13-14oz)) sugar depending on how sweet you want it
2 tsps citric acid
2 tsps tartaric acid
1 litre (2.2 pints) water

Pare away the rind of the lemons from the pith using a lemon zester. Juice the lemons and put this into a bowl with the sugar, tartaric and citric acid. Bring the water and the lemon rind to the boil and simmer for 3 minutes. Remove from the heat and strain the water over the juice and sugar mixture. Stir well to dissolve the sugar, straining again if necessary. Pour into bottles, storing them in a cool place for up to 4 weeks and chilling well before drinking.

Precycle!

Orange Barley Water

Barley water was traditionally made as a soothing drink for invalids in the Middle- Ages, but my main memory of barley water is the commercially produced one at Wimbledon each year. You can use any fruit as a base for barley water; lemons oranges, melons, strawberries.

You Will Need:

50g (2oz) pearl barley
500g (1 pint approx.) water
the juice and zest of two oranges
1-2 tbsps sugar depending on how sweet you like it, or try a tablespoon of honey.

Blanche and clean the barley by pouring boiling water over it. Place all the ingredients in a pan and simmer very gently for 20 minutes. Strain and leave it to cool before drinking. This beverage does not keep well so make only sufficient to be consumed in 24 hours.

Summer Fruit Punch

You Will Need:

200g (7oz) strawberries, hulled and quartered
100g (3½ oz) raspberries, hulled
50g (2oz) stoned cherries
the juice of 3 oranges
100g (3½ oz) sugar
1 litre (2.2 pints) water
1 litre (2.2 pints) white grape juice

Put the water and sugar into a pan and bring to the boil.

Place the fruit in a serving bowl and pour over the hot syrup. Leaveit to cool and add the juice of the oranges and the grape juice. Add plenty of ice just before serving. You can add as much brandy or white wine as you wish if you prefer your punch with a 'punch.'

Pineapple Cooler

You Will Need:

1 can of crushed pineapple
1 carton of fresh pineapple juice
the juice of 1 lime
2 tbsps powdered coconut milk, mixed with 4 tbsps warm water
100ml (a cupful) sparkling water or soda water
plenty of ice

Pour all the ingredients into a jug, except for the water and ice. Whisk for a few seconds using a hand blender to blend the pineapple. Add the water, the ice and perhaps a straw, a cherry on a stick or an umbrella and just enjoy it.

Summer beverages don't have to be alcoholic, but the next recipe is for an old favourite; good old homemade ginger beer, or root beer. It was particularly popular with farm workers during harvest time and can be drunk cold, but is still delicious and thirst quenching if it gets a little warm. You will need a sterile brewing bucket and glass bottles. The amount of bottles will depend on their size. Using bottles with reinforced corks is advisable as ginger beer has a habit of blowing its corks, so do take great care after the bottling stage. This recipe is also brilliant mixed with equal quantities of cold tea.

Precycle!

Ginger Beer

You Will Need:

20g (1oz) root ginger, grated
1 unwaxed lemon, juiced and zested
400g (13oz) sugar
4 litres (8 pints) water
20g (1 oz) cream of tartar
20g (1 oz) brewing yeast

Put the ginger, sugar, cream of tartar and lemon zest into a brewing bucket which will hold 9-10 litres and boil the water. This can be done in batches in the kettle. Pour it over the ginger mixture, add the lemon juice and stir well.

Allow it to cool until just warm and cream the yeast with a little liquid from the bucket. Stir it into the ginger liquid and cover. Leave it in a warm place for 24 hours before skimming off the froth without disturbing the sediment.

Using a jug, carefully pour the ginger beer into strong glass beer bottles, leaving a gap at the top, and cork each bottle. Store them in a cool place and check regularly. The corks may need to be released if fermentation is vigorous. The beer will be ready in 2-3 days.

I also like to make fruit and herb infusions that may be drunk warm or cold. They are very light and refreshing and, although they don't have a strong flavour, they do quench your thirst.

Lemon and Ginger

You Will Need:

the grated zest of ½ a lemon
the juice 1 lemon
¼ tsp crushed ginger
1 tsp honey

To make a mug of this put all ingredients into a small jug and fill it full of boiling water. Stir it well and allow it to steep for 5-6 minutes before drinking.

Lavender and Chamomile

You Will Need:

4 lavender flowers
1 chamomile tea bag or 5 chamomile flower heads
2 tbsps home made blackcurrant syrup
boiling water

Put the flowers and/or teabag into a small teapot and pour over sufficient boiling water to fill a mug. Stir well and leave to brew for 10 minutes. Add the syrup and fill your favourite mug with this soothing drink, straining away the flowers.

Precycle!

Home

Brewing

Beginners' Beers, Wines and Mead

Thirst is a terrible thing and, whereas you can get beer very cheaply, you will bc doing the planet a huge favour by making your own. For a start the packaging and bottling of beers is very costly in terms of energy, and therefore pollution, and the transportation of wine and beer certainly releases a lot of CO_2 into the atmosphere – as much as five times the amount released in the brewing proces itself. It can be argued that brewing beer and wine is carbon neutral and that any carbon released came from sugar that was initially collected from the atmosphere in the first place. The boiling of water also uses energy, and this is costly in both energy and pollution terms.

About 5000 years ago, when the UK was in the middle of what we now call the Iron Age, a number of cultures around the world more or less simultaneously invented ale. When you take grain, crush it and add a little water

Precycle!

and yeast it becomes bread. If you soak the grain and allow the starch to convert into sugar, the same yeast produces ale. That's all you have to do, but the leap forward to realising that soaking grain becomes sweet was an immense step forward for human technology.

Wine had been known for many thousands of years prior to this, so the art of fermentation was already well understood. Fermenting grain, however, was totally new. Beer is simply flavoured ale and, in the 13th century, the flavouring of choice was hops, and that choice has pretty much stuck ever since. The grains used are mostly barley, but wheat, corn and other seeds have also been used.

Malting

The basic principle is to steep grain in water so that it starts to grow. Enzymes in the seed then convert the insoluble starch into soluble sugar. At this point, because it is usually barley, we call the material malted barley. This is then put into a vessel and cooked to kill the plants. The flavourings are added and the liquid is then called wort. This is then yeasted and allowed to ferment. That's all there is to it!

If you allow the beer to ferment until all the sugar is used up you will get a strong beer and the yeast will die. The discovery that the viscosity of the liquid changes as the sugar is converted to alcohol made it possible to measure exactly how much alcohol is in the brew, and then to stop the brewing accordingly at the desired strength. A hydrometer is a standard sized bubble of a known weight. This floats in the beer and you can read off the number on the side. There is a formula that converts this number to the alcohol content, but we'll leave that for a later issue.

The brewing is stopped by adding Camden tablets, which release sulphur dioxide into the brew to kill the yeast.

Ancient British Ale

You will have realised that, in order to brew ale, you will need grain and 5000 years ago we didn't really grow much grain for baking, let alone drinking. But we did have honey, and there is evidence from the late Iron Age, and from the time of the arrival of the Romans, that we made ale with common weeds and honey.

Dandelion Beer from Honey

1kg (2.2lbs) whole dandelion plants,
including the flowers and the roots
1kg (2.2lbs) honey
the juice of a lemon
brewer's yeast

Wash the dandelions and boil them with the lemon juice. Add to 5 litres (a gallon) of cold water in a fermentation vessel. In this case a demijohn will do.

Ferment to 1.010 on the hydrometer and stop the process with a couple of Camden tablets. Or just ferment it until it stops bubbling if you are new to this.

Keep a few weeks before drinking. It is almost like wine and is not what you might recognise as beer today.

Beer From a Kit

Now I know I am going to get into trouble here. Some of you will start fretting about the kit itself. "It can't be organic or natural if it comes out of a tin, can it?" Some of you will get all upset about what I am going to say about lager and probably the kit manufacturer will get all upset with what I am about to do with it. But there is nothing wrong with learning about brewing by using a kit. You are provided with everything you need and all you have to add is sugar and water. Lots of water, in fact, in a large bucket. When I was a student we bought a dustbin in which we made brown ale. The bin was sterilised and filled monthly, and we eventually got to a point where our student flat had four dustbins all working away. We had a lot of friends.

Beer from a kit has a tin around it, and quite a large one at that to hold the hops. Rather than recycling this there are a number of things you can do. I have a drain pipe on my greenhouse that is fed from a gutter which is all made from beer kit tins. They also make great plant pots and super measurers. A small hole in the base will turn it into a great drip waterer too and needless to say they make brilliant targets, goal posts and, in one emergency, doubled up with limited success as a makeshift car exhaust.

New Dandelion Beer

This is based on a recipe that is many centuries old. It originally called for malted barley and dandelions as a flavouring but, to save all the boiling, and most people probably do not have enough space or equipment anyway, we are going to use the blandest beer kit there is. And what could be blander than lager, in my opinion? (At this point my editor advised me to add, 'in my opinion.' It was only added under duress!)

The beer kit is little more than wort in a tin. You can get organic beer kits if you like. Most of them contain no preservatives or nasty chemicals, just beer juice. Then you add boiling water to dissolve the thick liquid and top it up to 25 litres (or 43 pints) with cold water. Somewhere in this process you also add a kilo of sugar as a food source, and finally the yeast itself.

If you add sucrose or ordinary packet sugar in any of its varied guises, you will get a funny flavoured beer. This is because glucose is a disaccharide (or double sugar), and when the yeast breaks it down you get the added bonus of a mixture of flavours. Buy glucose from the chemist in the same quantity – usually 1kg (2lbs approx.). You will then get a beer that tastes like pub-bought, only-better.

In order to add the old, traditional flavour to the beer we are going to add a couple of litres of boiling dandelion water. Since lager is blandish (in fact the nearest beer there is to tea you can get - in my opinion), the dandelion will add an interesting flavour, closer to golden bitter than anything else.

Follow the recipe on the can, but the first boiling water should be made by collecting 2 very large handfuls of dandelion leaves boiled for ten minutes in the water. This is then strained into the fermentation vessel. The wort is added, then the sugar (don't forget, you're using glucose!), the rest of the water and the yeast, and away you go!

One last note. Brewing is a culture where you are growing yeast. The alcohol produced becomes a preservative, but you can also grow bacteria and unwanted fungi in the brew, so make sure that everything is sterile each time before use. The best way of doing this is with Milton or any good sterilising tablets, diluted appropriately.

In warm weather this brews well outside on the shelves in the garden. It takes about two weeks and then the beer can be siphoned into bottles or directly into a pressure vessel, so it can be poured off like draught beer.

Rich Dark Beer

There are two ways of making this; the easy and the hard way. The easy way is to buy a beer kit and adapt it. The hard way is to buy hops and boil them in a pan of water, then use the wort, which is what we call the liquid from the boiling mash. A beer kit, especially a good one, is simply the hard bit done for you by someone else.

You Will Need:

A 20 litre (4.5 gallon) dark beer kit
1kg (2.2lbs) dextrose (or glucose, which is the same thing)
1kg (2.2lbs) brown sugar
500g (1lb) raisins

Follow the instructions in the beer kit, but do not use sucrose for the main sugar, use dextrose. This gives a much better flavour. Then we are going to add more ordinary brown sugar. This will give the beer real strength.

Put 1 litre of water (about 2 pints) into a large pan with the raisins. Bring to the boil and simmer for 10 minutes. Strain the liquid into your wort and then bring it up to 20 litres (4.5 gallons).

I prefer to brew in a pressure vessel and pour from there, but this beer is best bottled. You can buy everything you need for making and bottling from a homebrew shop.

Leave the beer to brew for the appropriate time, which is really more of an art than a science. Since we have added more sugar and raisin juice to the brew, the specific gravity will not be exactly as recommended in the brewing kit. Indeed, it will be much stronger. After a fortnight I usually taste the beer every few days when it seems ready, which means that it isn't so yeasty and not so sweet. Then I siphon the beer into plastic fizzy pop bottles to finish the fermentation process.

Beer From First Principles

You Will Need:

1kg (2.2lbs) dark dried malt extract
450g (1lb approx.) light dried malt extract
125g (4oz) goldings hops
1kg (2.2lbs) brown sugar
1.4kg (3lbs) white sugar
beer yeast

Boil the ingredients, except for the sugar in a large pan with a gallon of water in it. Simmer for 30 minutes and strain into the fermenting vessel. Wash the hops out with a couple of kettles of boiling water. Make it up to 20 litres (around 4½ gallons) with cold water and dissolve the sugar into this. Sprinkle the yeast onto the liquid and then leave for a fortnight.

I then transfer this to my pressure vessel and simply forget about it. You can bottle it as above if you wish, but I don't bother. Add a spoon full of sugar to each bottle which brings on a secondary fermentation and gives the beer a good head.

For both these beers it is best to leave them for as long as you can. Bottled they should last for ten years or more, but I have never managed to test this.

Precycle!

Wines

Making country wines is a most fascinating process, and one which has served mankind for many hundreds, if not thousands, of generations, providing water in a safe drink, free from both diseases and nasties. Country wines are a celebration of the fruits and plants that created them. There is nothing easier than making wine and you can achieve some truly expert flavours. Sometimes the result can be a little harsh, but if you persevere you will become an expert. The most important thing in making wine is to remember that everything needs to be sterile and that the lees, or what is left by the dead yeast, tastes nasty, so you need the patience to draw off your wine (a process called racking) many times. The other thing to remember is that the wine needs time. We often expect chemistry to be instant, but the chemistry in a bottle of wine is a slow process, both complex and subtle. If you brew it one week and drink it the next you are not going to get good quality. Be patient. This way you will be able to compete with even the most expensive wines.

To ferment wine you need two jars, each about a gallon in size, a rubber bung with an airlock in place to let the gas escape while keeping oxygen from the air out, and some flavouring; fruit juice, half a bag of sugar, and a teaspoon of brewers yeast. You will need somewhere warm to start your wine, which can take a couple of weeks, and somewhere to store it after it is finished. You will also need a tube for siphoning it from one vessel to another, but that's all!

It is extremely important that everything you use to make wine is sterile. You don't want to be growing any microbes you don't need. Use sterilising tablets to disinfect glassware (demijohns, tubes, airlocks etc.) and boiling water for everything else.

You will need to collect enough fruit, flowers and leaves to make a gallon (4.5 litres) of juice. Collect only the best fruit, leaving anything bad or rotted behind and place it into muslin, tying this off to make a bag. Pour in two kettles full of boiling water and mash away with a potato masher or a rolling pin and leave the fruit to soak. Repeat the mashing and soaking until the liquid has cooled and then squeeze the muslin bag to remove all the concentrated juice.

You can add sugar to this juice, depending on how much sugar the juice already contains. You can measure the specific gravity of the liquid and get a reasonable idea of how much sugar it already contains, but as a rule of thumb with sweet fruit such as grapes or strawberries I add an extra 250g (8oz) of sugar and for more tart wines such as rhubarb I add an extra 500g (1lb).

Rinse all your equipment with cooled, boiled water and pour all your crushed fruit juice into the demijohn. Carefully top up with your syrup until it comes to the neck of the glass. Make sure the hot liquid does not touch the glass directly or it might crack.

Give it a shake and then add a teaspoon of brewer's yeast to the liquid. You don't need to start the yeast off or anything fancy – just plonk it in. Put a little water in the airlock and set it into position. Within a day the water in the airlock will be bubbling away as the fermentation starts. Don't worry about your juice bubbling up, or even hitting the bottom of the cork.

When the bubbling stops, around a fortnight later, transfer the wine from its brewing vessel to a second demijohn using a siphon tube. Be careful not to include any of the yeast that has gathered in the bottom. The process of siphoning the wine is called racking. This separates the wine from the dead yeast which will spoil the flavour if left too long.

Precycle!

Give the wine a good shake in its new demijohn. All the gas will come out of it. This is an important step because it allows the remains of the yeast in the wine to fall to the bottom, and the liquid will gradually clear. A few days later, if you can manage to wait that long, rack the wine again back into its original and now clean demijohn, this time avoiding the smaller film of yeast on the bottom.

By now you should have a pretty clear wine ready to drink. Purists will say that you have to bottle the wine to keep it, and you can siphon it into bottles and leave it to mature. Ever ready to economise I buy two 2 litre bottles of lemonade from the supermarket and pour the lemonade into a jar for immediate use which leaves me with two sterile bottles ideal for storing wine. You don't need to keep wine in glass or stoneware – plastic is actually just as good.

Raspberry Wine

In the late summer we collect around a hundred pounds of raspberries from the wild. Most of this is destined to become wine!

You Will Need:

2 kg (5lb approx.) raspberries
1kg (2lb approx.) sugar
1 tsp wine yeast
1 vitamin C tablet or some rosehip juice (to help
the yeast get going!)

Place the fruit into a muslin bag in a bucket and add a kettle of boiling water. Then bash away with a masher. When you are sure you have extracted all the juice, allow it to cool and filter it into the demijohn using another muslin bag.

Make a syrup with 1 litre of boiling water and sugar and allow it to cool. Add it to the demijohn. Top up with boiled, cooled water and add a teaspoon of yeast.

Elderflower Champagne

There are some prerequisites for a summer evening. Firstly, there must be night scented stocks, the final song of the skylark, the fluttering hum of the first pipistrelle as it hunts for moths, the complete intoxication of elder flower champagne and just maybe a couple of fairies. The elder is a magical plant. If you fall asleep under its branches, beware! You might just be pulled into fairy-land, never to be seen again. To our ancestors the wood of the elder was not for burning and, should it be dug up, the tree would have to be placated first.

The elder, or sambucus nigra, is a shrubby plant that has a grey bark and rather unpleasant smelling leaves. The flowers that appear in the spring are large, fluffy umbels. They appear after the blackthorn in hedges in the spring. The aroma of the flowers is amazing and they are quickly pollinated and go off. When the flowers turn yellow they also start to smell of cat and should be discarded.

They have been used as a tonic for many hundreds of years. The flowers and, to a greater extent the fruit, are rich in vitamin C. Elderflower tea has been used for ages as a pick me up when you have a cold. There are a number of studies looking at the efficacy of elderflower and arthritis but it is too soon to say if it has any effect.

The plant is rather high in tannins and has to be processed before consumption. The flowers and fruit are usually doused in boiling water before being made into drinks. The fruit is also cooked in pies. Do not try to eat more than one or two of the berries; apart from being very sour they will also give a blistering bellyache.

Do not attempt to eat the leaves at all and do not feed

Precycle!

them to your livestock. If you do the fairies will definitely come to pay you a visit in the night!

Elderflower is only viable on the plant for a couple of days. If you can smell the flowers then so can every insect in the county. The flowers are pollinated very quickly. Collect only the white florets that smell crisp and look clean. Give them a good shake to dislodge any wildlife. Use the flowers quickly after collecting them and make sure you do not take all of them, otherwise there will be no elderberries in the late summer. And always pick them when the sun is out, making sure they are dry and fully open.

Strong Elderflower Champagne

You Will Need:

4 large elderflower florets
200ml (6fl oz) or 1 small can white wine base (This gives extra body and can be bought from homebrew suppliers)
1kg (2.2lbs) ordinary white sugar (Using dextrose does not help the flavour as it does beer, so use the ordinary stuff)
5g (1 tsp) citric acid
1 cup of strong tea
wine yeast

Strip the flowers off their stalks with a fork into a sterile bucket. Pour over 5 litres (about a gallons) of boiling water and stir regularly over a 24 hour period.

Dissolve the sugar into 500ml (1 pint) of boiling water to make a sugar syrup. Strain the cooled liquid into a second bucket through a muslin and add the sugar syrup. Transfer to a demijohn and add all the other ingredients, giving the vessel a good shake to mix them well.

If the demijohn needs to be topped up, use cooled

boiled water. Close the vessel with an airlock and stand it on a tray in case the wine spills out when the fermentation starts. When the bubbling has stopped, siphon off the liquid into a clean, sterilised demijohn, leaving the gunge behind in the bottom of the vessel. Top up with either apple juice or boiled water. Close the new vessel off with an airlock.

Leave to stand for about six months (if you can bear to) and then rack it off into bottles.

Mild Elderflower Champagne

You Will Need:

6 elderflower heads
the juice and pulp of 2 lemons
4 litres (1 gallon approx.) of water
750g (1lb 8oz) sugar

Put the elderflower heads and the lemon pulp in a bucket and pour on the boiling water. Leave it to soak for 24 hours covered with a tea towel. Strain through a muslin and add the sugar and lemon juice. Stir until the sugar is completely dissolved and pour into two 2 litre screwtop lemonade bottles. Leave the tops slightly loose for a couple of weeks. Keep for 2 to 3 months before drinking. Serve chilled on a hot summer evening.

Making Mead

Mead is made in the same way as wine, or at least when it is made in small quantities. It used to be made in large skins, but you can certainly make a gallon very easily. Remember that honey is about 80% sugar, which means that you need to add more than you would if making wine from sugar. The sweet, sticky stuff sold as mead is a nonsense. It was the wedding drink of the Vikings and

Precycle!

this is the very best way to imagine it.

You Will Need:

1.25kg (3lbs approx.) honey
4.5 litres (1 gallon) water
1 tbsp white wine yeast
2 lemons

Bring the water to the boil and allow it to cool. Add the honey and pour the mixture into the demijohn, adding a tablespoon of white wine yeast. Then add the juice of the 2 lemons.

Add an air lock and forget about it. The process takes a long time to work. When the bubbles stop, which can take up to a month, rack it off into a clean demijohn and, if you can, stand it on a stone floor as the vibrations from around the house can make wooden floors wobble, which can mix up your mead. Rack a couple of times when the sediment settles. Mead is a slow chemistry brew. It will take a year to achieve its best flavour, so try to leave it as long as you can.

Household Cleaners

Bleach, Polishes and Soaps

Messing about with chemicals is dangerous! Don't do anything you are not completely sure about. Always wear protective clothing such as an apron, glasses and gloves. Always have a lot of water available to drench yourself with if it all goes wrong and never mix chemicals unless you know what is going to happen And finally, never, ever, lick your fingers.

Don't mix mains electricity and liquid of any kind and never heat chemicals, especially bleach, vinegar, oils, fuels or anything else for that matter. You have been warned! Messing about with things you know nothing about can ruin your day, week, year or even your life!

Whatever did we do before the days of bleach and disinfectant? In the ordinary kitchen there are now more than ten different types of cleaner, from bleach to cream cleansers which, by the way, do not have any cream in them whatsoever. Their purpose seems to be to protect us in the ongoing war with a bacterial culture, our earlier

Precycle!

resistance to which these same cleaners have probably been single-handedly responsible for destroying.

There are now disinfectants for carpets, for work surfaces, for sinks and drains, some with and some without fragrance, some even designed to neutralise odours, and some for use with scourers and some not to protect our lovely shiny surfaces.

It is interesting to note that for years we have been soaking our houses with chemicals that are often now deemed too dangerous for human health. There has been a drive to check almost every chemical in human existence for the last twenty years. We no longer have phenols and many benzene products, although trichlorophenylmethyliodosalicyl (TCP to you and me!) is still available as a solution of chlorinated phenols. Trichlorophenol is no longer used except as a fungicide. But this massive and volatile range of chemicals that have been the very backbone of keeping us free from germs for generations are now being replaced by a new set of safer ones, or so we are told.

Certainly we did used to disinfect our homes with some very strong chemicals. We are told that modern disinfectants are milder on the skin while at the same time being more effective on harmful bacteria. However, we live in an age where hospitals have rampant 'superbug' problems. The growth of many of these superbugs is related to the behaviour of people rather than the efficiency of our chemicals. The disinfecting methods of a hundred years ago still work well today, and this is the basis on which we shall progress in the next section.

There is plenty of anecdotal and scientific evidence to suggest that modern cleaning methods are not as good as those of yesteryear. Sometimes we rely on chemicals to replace hard work (see the Mr. Muscle adverts) and at the same time overlook the fact that the pristine nature of our homes is actually affecting the immune systems of our children.

On the other hand noone wants to return to the bad old days of terrible water borne infections such as typhoid and unsanitary homes.

A little bit about Sodium Hypochlorite

Sodium Hypochlorite is the mainstay of antibacterial and antifungal disinfecting. It is found in most products as a solution in brine called Dakin's solution. Dakin was an American who studied the electrolysis of salt solution to create hypochlorite. Almost every schoolboy will tell you that if you pass an electric current through a solution of salt you will get hydrogen and oxygen. But you also get other chemicals such as chlorine and sodium hydroxide, and if these combine they produce the disinfecting hypochlorite ion.

Sodium hypochlorite is also known as bleach and high concentrations can be both powerful and damaging, so it should only be used in weak dilutions. It is never sold in concentrations greater than 5%, and even at this strength it is really powerful stuff. For ordinary disinfecting you only need a 0.1% solution and this is easy to make at home.

The easiest way to make a disinfecting solution is to copy Milton, which is a British product. Add a dessert spoon of bleach and four dessert spoons of salt to 1 litre of water (2.2 pints). This will produce a safe solution for disinfecting worktops which will have a mild bleaching action. It will, however, still spoil your clothes if it splashes over you.

You can also make your own hypochlorite. It occurs

Precycle!

when you pass a current through a brine solution and I do it in an old car battery. You can get car batteries from the dump and they will dispose of the acid for you. It must be a working battery, which you can charge up with solar or wind power if you like. The empty battery needs washing out with many gallons of water.

Pour a 3% salt solution into the battery. It will hold about 5 litres, so that is 150g of salt. Then connect the working battery to the salt filled one with jump leads and leave it in a safe, well ventilated place. After about 2 hours you will have a solution of hypochlorite and salt of the required strength.

It is not possible to say exactly how strong this material is. This will depend on many variables, including the efficiency of your power battery. Compare the aroma (don't get a nose full, just a slight whiff), to the shop bought stuff and always use it very sparingly.

MAKE SURE YOU TAKE PRECAUTIONS IF YOU DECIDE TO MAKE THIS SUBSTANCE! Do not electrocute yourself and be certain that you are quite sure what you are doing and that you are able to remain safe all the time. DO NOT USE A MAINS BATTERY CHARGER FOR THIS PROCESS!

Salt (a bit of an aside!)

It might be a coincidence, but the concentration of salt in seawater is exactly the same as in our blood; a fact that has driven evolutionary scientists mad over the years. The point is that evaporated seawater makes a salt that quite closely resembles our own chemistry. Of course, a trip to the seaside can provide you with salt by evaporating seawater in a large dish.

A gallon of seawater will contain somewhere between 100 and 200g of dry matter, mostly sodium chloride, but

Household Cleaning Products

with plenty of other chemicals too like magnesium. But this is only a few times the recommended daily allowance of salt, so you will need a lot of seawater to make it in sufficient quantities for a family.

An alternative to this kind of salt is to dry vegetables in the oven very slowly until they are paper dry. These can be ground to a dust and combined to make a powder. Good combinations are onion and nettle leaves. This isn't salt, but it does contain salt.

Another way of creating a good alternative is to collect seaweed, dry it to a powder and grind it to a dust. This is actually quite salty and is also good for you. Any of the green or brown seaweeds will do the job well. Please don't take red seaweeds from the beach, though, because many of them are quite rare.

All Purpose Cleaner

A mixture of equal volumes of bicarb and white vinegar together with ten times the volume of water. We will see later that this is the fundamental basis for cleaners that disinfect, remove grease and clean all surfaces. Of course, the bicarb breaks down when the acid is added and this is what makes the cleaner work so well. Put it in a spray bottle and use it to clean glass, metal, wood, work surfaces and in fact anything. Add a tablespoon of salt and the juice of a lemon for both fragrance and extra disinfecting properties. You can make a gallon of this cleaner for much less than the very cheapest washing up liquid available.

Precycle!

Cream Cleaner

A cream cleaner is designed to wipe ceramic tops with a degree of abrasion. This is provided by combining kaolin and some liquid or other, often a mixture of a weak solution of soap with a small amount of sodium hydroxide. But just because there is such a thing as a cream cleanser doesn't meanthat you have to use it. A simple spray of a disinfectant solution as described previously and a sprinkle of salt is just as good, if not better.

How Salt Cleans and Disinfects

Water is important for life. Salt has a greater affinity for water than even our own tissues and certainly the cells of bacteria and fungi. If you have a strong enough solution of salt it will pull out water from living cells, killing them in the process. There is no bug around that can withstand this. So, if you dampen your worktop with a dilute bleach, the microbes will have their cell walls severely weakened by the hypochlorite as it burns through and the sprinkling of salt will then dissolve in the film, making a really strong solution. If you leave this for a few minutes and wipe it clean with a clean cloth, you will have a perfectly clean and sterile surface.

The Importance of Vinegar

Created from alcohol, vinegar is a simple molecule with a huge potential in the modern home. Its only drawback is the smell, but it is such a common chemical that we are almost all used to handling it. True, it is a little harsh on the skin, but the appropriate use of rubber gloves easily removes that problem.

The scientifically minded among you will appreciate that vinegar is an unbalanced molecule. It has delocalised electrons whizzing around at one end but not the other and this gives the molecule similar properties to water, but rather more pronounced. Bear in mind that electrons are reactive and you have a molecule that, if it cannot dissolve something, will chemically react with it. Fortunately most vinegars we have are very mild in their reactivity and perfectly safe for humans. However, it is poisonous to many bacteria, and its affinity for water acts like salt. In other words, it makes a very good disinfectant.

You can use vinegar as a general disinfecting cleaner. Simply add 1 quarter of the volume of liquid soap (homemade or otherwise) in the form of four tablespoons of vinegar topped up with water and two level teaspoons of salt. You can use this neat with a cloth to disinfect and clean most surfaces.

Where you need to clean up more unsightly problems caused by pets, children and sometimes adults (blunders, we call them), neat vinegar will not only make the material safe to handle, especially if sprinkled with salt first, but the aroma of vinegar will also reduce the odour of the blunder, whatever it might be. One day, while engaged in such a task, I found myself wondering whether the chemicals in the disinfectant I was using and the cleaner afterwards, were actually worse for the planet and the people who live in the house than those left behind by the puppy. Since that time I have only used natural chemicals to clean up so-called blunders.

Vinegar will dissolve grease so, for non-detergent washing of pots, use very hot water and an egg cup full of vinegar. The hot water will melt the grease but the vinegar will remove it from the water, allowing you to clean them more easily.

Vinegar adds a sparkle to glass and crystal washing. Just add a small amount to the final rinse and allow them to dry naturally. Similarly, wash a cup with half a teaspoon of salt and a tablespoon of vinegar to remove ground in tea and coffee stains and your final result will be more resilient to staining.

You can use the electrons in vinegar to absorb static electricity. Why would you want to do this? Well, a wash of a gallon of water, a squirt of soap and half a cup of vinegar around the house will cut down your dust accumulation problem considerably.

Because we are able to take vinegar in our diets, especially on salads, it is possible to use it as a purifier, particularly of bottled water. All you need are a couple of drops of vinegar in a pintof water or no more than three per litre and the bottled water will keep fresher for longer, as much as a week longer. It is also good to use when you take water from fast flowing rivers as an extra backup. But this will not make very contaminated water safe to drink so any water you are concerned about should also be boiled.

Vinegar and any oil in equal measure makes for a brilliant stain remover. It works on wood because, whereas the vinegar would react with the varnish, any tarnish is dealt with by the oil. So stains on wood can be rubbed away with this mixture quite easily. The same goes for dealing with horrid stuff like chewing gum (although this takes quite a bit of work) and the glue from labels left behind when you try to remove them from gifts. (Why they do this I don't know, but it is infuriating!).

Of course, vinegar is a mild acid and has a pH of around 4, which means it is ten thousand times milder than mineral acids and a thousand times more acid than water. A solution of a tablespoon of vinegar to a pint of water will remove the fur left behind by hard water on pottery and inside a kettle. It will also prevent corrosion of your washing machine if, once a month, you add half a cup to a wash load to help remove the limescale.

Sink and Bathroom Cleaner

This brings us on to the use of borax and bicarb in the home. For a thousand years and more borax has been used to disinfect and clean because it is antibacterial, antifungal and kills insect infestations with ease.

Bicarb, or bicarbonate of soda, is a more modern invention, being merely a few hundred years old. Its action is chemical. It reacts with acid to release carbon dioxide and, when these reactions take place, there are a lot of ionic particles that disrupt both grease and dirt.

An excellent sink and bathroom cleaner can be made from equal quantities (a teaspoon of each) of borax, bicarb and water. To improve its disinfecting qualities you can add a teaspoon of salt.

But beware! BORAX IS POISONOUS. A teaspoonful is enough to kill, so do not use it near food. Wear gloves and do not inhale it. Having said that it has been used for many years, converting water to hydrogen peroxide which in turn bleaches the surface.

A Detergent Alternative

If you collect small remnant pieces of soap and mix them with an equal weight of bicarb, dissolving them in the minimum amount of boiling water you can get away with, then two tablespoons of this is enough for a washer full of clothes.

Precycle!

Ever Handy Washing Soda

If you want to cut down on the chemistry within your cleaning cupboard, keep just the following: soap, washing soda, bicarb, vinegar, salt and water. This is the total toolkit needed to keep your house both clean and disease free.

Washing Soda is sodium carbonate and has, for centuries, been used as a cleaning and disinfecting agent. When you buy washing powder you are buying mostly washing soda with additives. Its sole real active ingredient is still good old fashioned washing soda.

This is the green alternative to all your detergents. You can soak clothes if you need deep stains removing, and it will work in any washing machine. It can also be used around the home and is the single best drain clearer you can buy. You don't really need anything else.

Fabric Conditioner

The modern fabric conditioners contain proteins that make your clothes feel soft. Most people tend to use them because they smell good. Well, you can make your own fabric conditioner that is easier on the environment as well as cheaper. Mix equal quantities (by volume) of bicarb and white vinegar. It will fizz like mad at first, but keep on mixing until it stops. Then dilute this with twice as much water and add 6 drops of your favourite essential oil. Use this in a similar quantity to bought conditioner in your rinse cycle.

Another great fabric conditioner is made from the juice of four lemons and a tablespoon of bicarb in a pint (half a litre) of water. This combination is virtually free from anything unnatural. Add it to your washing for the spin cycle as you would with a bought product.

A lot of people also want to keep their clothes free from static cling. This can be done by drying them on a washing line or by drip drying, but when you have to use a dryer simply remove them from the dryer with wet hands. There is no need to buy anything special. The static will be 'absorbed' by the dipole in the water molecules.

Ironing Fragrances

People like to add a fragrance to the steam iron, and this is easy enough to replicate. Fill a cleaned out detergent bottle with water and add 1 teaspoon of washing soda and a few lavender heads. If you haven't got lavender try sweet pea flowers. Use this water to fill your iron. It is every bit as good as any bought product.

Ironing Starch

Buy a spray bottle, add a tablespoon of cornflower and fill the bottle with water. Give it a good shake and allow a couple of hours for it to dissolve; there will always be a little powder at the bottom. Use this as a mild starch-when necessary.

Air Fresheners

You can't beat fresh air! Open a window, it's so much better than filling the atmosphere with all kinds of problematic molecules. You also have to remember that bad smells tend to accumulate because of a need to clean. I am not being rude here but if you fry fish your house will smell and you will need to do something about it.

It also has to be said that if you fill your house with plants, any aromas will disperse more quickly than otherwise. This is because plants actively transpire chemicals from the atmosphere as well as having their own distinctive smells. There is a world of difference between masking a smell and absorbing it. We shall concentrate on absorption. Why should we fill a room with chemicals?

If you have been painting, cut a few onions and leave them on plates around the room. The petroleum based molecules will react with the sulphur based molecules in the onion. Similarly, a mixture of bicarb and lemon juice on a saucer will absorb many smells. Atomised vinegar, made by boiling a tablespoon of vinegar in a pan of water, will absorb fishy smells. Boiling cinnamon and other herbs will do the same.

Oven Cleaner

Bicarb makes a great oven cleaner so don't bother to buy any of those powerful cleaners that will probably take off all your skin off if you touch them. Simply mix a cup of washing soda and a tablespoon of salt and work into a paste with half the volume of water. You need to let the paste work on the oven overnight and then clean it off the following day with a cloth and some water.

Carpet Cleaner

For mild stains keep a spray bottle with a 50% water and 50% white vinegar mix. Spray a small amount and then wipe with a cloth. For bigger more difficult stains use a mixture of equal quantities of borax, salt and water to make a paste. Scrub this paste into the stain, allow it to dry and vacuum or brush it up when dry.

Wax Furniture Polish

The best furniture polish is without doubt beeswax. Simply put equal volumes of beeswax and turpentine in a sealable container and allow a week for it to slowly dissolve. Apply with a soft cloth and buff with a second, softer cloth.

Homemade Shoe Polish

You have to remember that shoe polish does not clean your shoes. Correctly cared for shoes are cleaned with a damp cloth with a little detergent if necessary. Then the shoes are polished. This can be done by using a little oil on a cloth, preferably olive oil, but almost any other oil will do the trick. Simply rub it in with a cloth and buff to a shine.

Furniture Polish and Other Cleaners

Polishing and cleaning antique furniture can be a complete financial disaster, so be careful what you do with the cleaning materials and polishes in this section. You should always test your cleaning technique and materials on a small and less visible part of the furniture first, before doing the whole job.

Polishes frequently come in sprays and cans these days and we often forget that they have actually been around for a long time. Polish as a spray is only so useful and is, in fact, usually more of a cleaning substance than a polish. Any oil can be used to create a fine surface that is reflective and shiny, but only beeswax makes a truly perfect protective polish.

The propellants in furniture polish always take my breath away and consequently I never use them. There is something I really like about using a cloth and dipping it in a polish rather than spraying the stuff all over the place.

To make beeswax polish you need beeswax (obviously) and turpentine in equal quantities. The best way to make it is to get 50ml (2oz) of turpentine and add beeswax in small quantities, stirring all the time. Keep it away from naked lights and wear rubber gloves. Stir the wax into the turpentine until it will dissolve no more and transfer the contents to a clean, dry jam jar and stand it in boiling water. Do this by boiling a kettle, pouring the hot water into a pan and then plunging the jam jar into this liquid. Rest the lid on the jar in order to keep the water out. Then add at least as much beeswax into the jam jar as you have already dissolved and stir it in as the mixture melts under the heat. If necessary, refresh the boiling water.

When the wax is melted close the lid and allow it to cool. Use this polish with a soft cloth on the wood with a circular motion, rubbing it in well and with some force. You can buff with a softer cloth afterwards.

A quick cleaning mixture can be made from what is in all respects none other than a salad dressing. Well, that's what it is! Mix 2 parts of olive oil and 1 part lemon juice in a bowl and use this to polish the wood. Because this is a cleaning mixture, the lemon juice will do a little bleaching and the oil will fill in the gaps between the wood grains. Use a toothbrush or a nail brush to get to ingrained areas. If the wood is very light then use sunflower oil instead of olive oil. Anything you have left you really can sprinkle on your salad.

To preserve virgin wood use equal amounts of sunflower oil, motor oil (new, fresh stuff, not straight from the sump!) and lemon juice. Use a brush to paint the material lightly onto the wood, wiping away any excess. This material can be replaced with a lighter mixture once the oil has soaked in. A really good finish can be achieved by finishing off with beeswax.This makes cheap wood last longer and dramatically improves the look.

Another deep cleaner for old wooden furniture is the application of equal quantities of olive oil and vinegar. This material will, when rubbed into dark stained areas, lift the grease that holds the grime into the wood. If the material is very old and badly stained, rub it gently with a mixture of 1 teaspoon of washing soda, 1 teaspoon of vinegar and 1 teaspoon of olive oil in 2 tablespoons of warm water.

Glassware

There are a number of ways to clean glassware that normal washing often misses. For a start, most water is packed with carbonates that leave a film on glassware. Secondly, glasses are so often left to dry before they are washed and this creates etched areas, especially where wine dregs are left.

Use chemistry to clean and clear your glasses. Simply put a teaspoon of bicarbonate of soda into the bottom of the glass and top it up with a 4:1 dilution of water and vinegar. The reaction that takes place leaving bubbles everywhere releases all kinds of chemicals, charged particles and reactions in the glass. This will clear the film. The same material can be used to descale a kettle.

Cleaning Grained or Stained Metal

Its is a truly difficult job when a stainless pan becomes stained by burned food and the mess stubbornly refuses to come off. You need a two pronged approach that uses a weed from the garden and olive oil. Pull (don't

Precycle!

cut because you will ruin your knife!) some equisetum (also known as mare's tail) from the garden. This plant is impregnated with microscopic silica particles. The plant used to be called Pots and Pans. Put some olive oil on the stain, which acts as a solvent, and then rub with some folded plant. It will become green but this will wash away. Keep up the work and within a few minutes the stain will be removed.

Window Cleaner

People spend a fortune on window cleaning materials that almost universally leave the window dirtier, or streakier, than before. All you need to use to clean windows is two tablespoons of washing soda and half a cup of vinegar to a bucket full of water. The non-foaming liquid will clean away the grease and the vinegar will stop the streaks. The best piece of equipment you can get is a squeegee for washing away the excess water. Buff the glass with old newspaper afterwards.

Emulsion Paint

You can make a really good paint with quark – a kind of cheese. It is an acidic cheese which is made by microbial action without rennet. A solution of cheese starter is added to milk and allowed to set, stirring all the time. Some of the whey is poured off and the rest is beaten until it forms a good emulsion. This can be dyed with all kinds of pigment.

This kind of paint is no good if the walls are damp because it will go off and will smell. But when the walls are dry the quark paint dries to become completely odourless. Don't worry if you cannot make quark cheese yourself; it is sold in tubs in most supermarkets.

Soap Making

Making soap can be either easy or hard, depending on whether you use basic ingredients such as fat and lye (sodium hydroxide or caustic soda) or whether you use glycerine soap and add your own special ingredients. Both methods have their own special pros and cons. Using lye is dangerous, which is why the British call it caustic soda. It is not only poisonous but also very corrosive and you can cause yourself serious injury. On the other hand, getting hold of glycerine soap can be difficult and costly, though you will find plenty of recipes for specialised soaps that are well worth buying the glycerine soap for.

There are many processes that produce soap. In effect you are adding an electron to fat and making it soluble, but it is a little more complex than that. The chemistry is called saponification and the purpose is to produce a fat that will dissolve substances such as grease and oil but is itself soluble in water so that you can get the grease out of your skin or clothes and wash the soap away.

It is thought by some that soap was created almost by accident in Roman times where, at Mount Sapo, they sacrificed animals. It is thought that a mixture of tallow and wood ash flowed into the river and women found it easier to clean their clothes in the water. However, there is little proof of the veracity of this tale.

Most modern detergents are not soap. They are very complex combinations of chemicals which eventually end up in our rivers. Soap is just fat that has been made soluble, but that still has the ability to dissolve fat in its structure. Detergents, however, often contain stabilisers, enzymes and lots of salt. If we all made our own soap thenour rivers would be much cleaner.

Precycle!

Cleaning Lye and Other Chemicals

If you pour neat lye down the drain you should expect it to have an environmental effect. When you dispose of spent chemicals, wash them away with as much water as you can afford. A tenfold dilution is much better for the environment than a simple quick rinse.

How to Make Lye

The strength of the lye is not that important because you can simply continue adding a weaker solution until all the fat has reacted. Also, you don't need sodium hydroxide in particular as any alkali will do. It is the hydroxide bit (OH) that does the work. So you can in fact make a generic lye that is a mixture of all sorts of things, but with enough OH to make soap. You need to burn plant material and then soak the ashes in water. It is this soaking that produces the solution.

Fix a tap to a 205 litre barrel, a few inches from the bottom. Fill it with a layer of bricks, then straw and then some stones. This makes a brilliant filter. Pile the barrel with ashes and cover them with water. The ashes will sink, so add more and more until it is full. Leave this to soak for 48 hours. You will need to wear protective clothing, gloves and goggles to do this.

The egg test is a really important one for all sorts of processes. For example, if you are making brine to soak a ham, if a raw egg floats in the solution it is strong enough. Similarly, if your fresh (un-boiled) egg floats in the lye solution, it is strong enough for soap making.

Although I really want to show you how to make all kinds of soap, I am not very interested in boiling lime in water and making all sorts of concoctions that are either too cumbersome or too downright dangerous to be achieved in the ordinary home. There are a large number of websites or books on the subject, should you have a self harming bent, or should you really need to know how to do it.

It is usually best if you render the fat in the first place. This means gently heating it to beyond the melting point of the various types of fat in the tissue. For pork you need to get the fat to about 90°C. This is best done in a slow oven with your piece of fat, available from any butcher, on a net or a grill. If the fat is smoking or spitting, turn the heat down as low as you can. In fact any fat that has melted and fallen into the pan can be used for soapmaking.

Simple Hard Soap

This takes all day to make and sometimes longer, but you can stop the process and start again in the morning and you don't have to use the strongest solution of lye. Do the egg test and if the egg sinks slowly, that's fine. You can buy lye and dilute it yourself. Make sure you protect yourself from any splashes. You need a large earthenware pot that will go in the oven. The oven should be on a low setting (100°C GAS mark ¼). Put equal amounts of lye and the fat of your choice (pork fat is good for this) and pop it in the oven. Use about 1kg or 2lbs of fat and a roughly similar amount of lye. Every 15 minutes give it a stir with a wooden spoon and add more lye in very small amounts as it is used up. You want a mixture that is just hot enough to boil but does not boil completely dry. Keep on looking at the mix every 15 minutes, giving it a stir and adding more lye if it looks as though it is drying out. About 8 hours of this will produce a lump of soap that you can mould. It is ready when the fat has all changed in nature and melted uniformly.

Precycle!

Laundry Soap

This is a generic recipe which will produce a powdered soap for the washing machine, or you can form it into a block if you wish.

You Will Need:

1 large enamelled pot
2.5kg (5lbs approx.) melted fat – beef is best for this one
300g (9oz) lye
6 cups of water
125g (4oz) borax
protective clothing

Melt your fat and heat your water until it is just above hand hot. Carefully add your lye and stir until it is all dissolved. Pour your fat into the large pot and slowly pour the lye mixture into the fat, stirring all the time. Sprinkle the borax into this mixture and stir it in until it is all absorbed. The soap will start to form over the next few hours and you should stir the coagulating mixture every 15 minutes or so for the rest of the day. The next morning and occasionally for the rest of the day you will need to continue to mash the mixture until it resembles porridge. It is now ready to dry out.

You can pour the soap into a mould and leave it to dry over the next couple of weeks. Alternatively, pour the mixture thinly on to silicone paper and allow it to dry out completely. This can take up to 2 weeks.

You can mill the dried soap in a mincing machine and this will give you flakes that you can use in the washing machine. Use it sparingly; a handful for each washer load will do the trick. I make sure I wash it down the drawer with some hot water. It doesn't create a huge lather, but it does do the job very well indeed..

Grated Green Soap for Washing Up

You can easily make your own soap from commercial laundry soap by grating it and dissolving it in boiling water. With the addition of washing soda and borax you will get a gel soap that you can use for washing up.

You Will Need:

100g (3½ oz) green soap block, grated
1 litre (2.2 pints) boiling water
125g (4oz) borax
125g (4oz) washing soda

Grate the soap into a bucket and add the boiling water. Stir until all the soap has dissolved and then mix in the borax and washing soda. Stir completely and leave to cool. The material should form a gel which, if it is too thick, can be dissolved with more boiling water. If you want to thicken this soap, add 2oz (50g) salt, although I have never felt this to be necessary.

Precycle!

Hair and Beauty

Soap, Shampoos, Cosmetics & Facials

Making soap from fat and alkali can be both messy and daunting, to say the least. The best thing about making soap from lye is that you can make yourself a few kilos for very little money. Indeed, this was the way soap was always made in the home until the mid-Victorian period when Lever Brothers started to make Sunlight Soap. You can still go to Port Sunlight, but it's a huge oil refinery now.

The Theory Behind Glycerine Soap

Glycerine is a by-product of the soap-making process. When you add lye to animal fat the glycerine pours off and is collected for the food industry. This is treated to make the soap and is then sold in either flakes or blocks. You can buy a large amount of soap flakes very cheaply and then use it to make your own speciality soaps which are often 20 times more expensive if bought from the shops!

Precycle!

To make your soap all you need is a double boiler in which to melt the flakes. You could, if you wanted, simply force the flakes into a bar but the real point of doing this is to create something with a little more panache.

Melt the flakes in a double boiler. I use a glass bowl over a pan of boiling water. When the soap is melted add your ingredients. If you wish to add colour you will need to experiment to get the right effect. If you are adding essential oils then six or seven drops should be enough, but try different amounts to get the correct balance. The last thing you need, though, is too concentrated a bar that actually hurts the skin.

For other ingredients work at increasing by 5% levels so that if you are adding salt, add 5%, i.e. a level teaspoonful per 100g of soap. If you are adding nutrients, use twice as much. Finally, if you are adding any other base, such as coconut oil or beeswax, then add 20%.

While the soap is still on the heat, mix everything with a spoon or a piece of wood. You can save your old lolly sticks for this task. Only pour off into your mould when you are happy that everything is properly mixed.

You will find that bubbles form in the soap when you add other ingredients. Skim them off with a spoon. This is a must if you are trying to make a clear bar of soap. I don't really worry about a few bubbles for home use but if it is for presents then perfection is a must.

The moulds do not need to be huge. These are rich soaps and you don't need a lot of them to be useful. If the mixture you have created refuses to set then re-melt it and add 5% salt. This will act as a thickener. If it still refuses to set you can re-melt and add more flakes, or even a sheet of cooking gelatine.

You can buy soap moulds of all different shapes and sizes. I find that plastic moulds are the best because the soap simply comes away from the inside. If you are feeling particularly lush you can use those silicone-baking trays, but then you won't be able to use them for food unless they get a really good wash.

You can also use ice-cube trays for soaps to take on holiday, or even household soap holders for a really big bar. The ice cube idea is excellent for people who make their own soap for health reasons because they are so easy to carry around.

The following recipes are included as they are useful both cosmetically and as an aid for the skin. You can make soaps for the hair, the skin, for fragrance and for presents.

Olive Oil, Oatmeal and Sea Salt Soap

These ingredients soften the skin and produce no irritation. The soap does not dry the skin, leaving it clean and soft. The oatmeal very slightly sloughs the skin and the sea salt, apart from making a hard bar, is a perfect cleanser.

You Will Need:

200g (6½ oz) glycerine soap
1 tsp sea salt
10ml olive oil (2 tbsps, but you can let your elbow
slip on this one)
20g (1oz approx.) fine oatmeal (for a more abrasive soap
use coarse oatmeal – some people use porridge oats)

Melt the soap. Add the olive oil first, then the salt and beat well. Then add the oatmeal and mix until all the oats are covered. Pour into moulds.

Precycle!

Lavender Oil, Coconut Oil and Thyme Soap

This soap calms the skin when it is irritated, for example when you have been out in the sun, or have a problem. The coconut oil cleanses and moisturises and the thyme and lavender are antibacterial.

You Will Need:

200g (6½ oz) glycerine soap
10g (⅓ oz) coconut oil (this comes in a solid block)
6/7 drops lavender oil
a small handful thyme leaves and flowers

Melt the soap and add the coconut oil. Then add the lavender drops and mix well. Sprinkle the thyme into the moulds and pour on the soap.

Honey, Lemon and Beeswax Soap

This is mild, moisturising and long lasting. The honey and beeswax have healing properties and this is a very luxuriant soap. The lemon not only smells good, but increases the acidity of the soap.

You Will Need:

200g (6½ oz) glycerine soap
30g (1oz) beeswax
10ml (2 tbsps) lemon juice
10ml (2 tbsps) honey

Mix the soap and beeswax and melt them together. Add the lemon juice, stirring all the time. Remove any scum from the surface and then add the honey. This solidifies as soon as you put it in the hot liquid but keep on stirring and it will slowly break into the mix. Pour into moulds. This soap is very rich and quite hard.

Tea Tree and Mint Soap

This cleanses the skin, is antibacterial and can help with problem skin. The mint cools and gives a pleasant odour which can also be good when you have a cold. It cleans your pores and leaves your skin feeling refreshed.

You Will Need:

200g (6½ oz) glycerine soap
6/7 drops tea tree oil
a small handful of mint leaves from the garden,
finely chopped

Melt the soap and add the tea tree oil and mint. Mix well and place some mint in the moulds. Pour into the moulds and allow to set slowly. This soap is very soft and aromatic.

Coconut Scrub

Coconut oil is great for moisturising, but desiccated coconut acts as an exfoliant. This is a great one for when your skin needs a retread.

You Will Need:

200g (6½ oz) glycerine soap
10g (⅓ oz) coconut oil
20g (⅔ oz) desiccated coconut

Melt the soap and add the other ingredients. Give the moulds a stir as they set to distribute coconut flakes evenly.

Precycle!

Rosemary and Henna Shampoo Bar

This is for dark hair, gives a great shine and is good for the scalp.

You Will Need:

200g (6½ oz) glycerine soap
3 tbsps rosemary infusion juice
20g (⅔ oz) henna powder

The infusion is made with a good handful of rosemary leaves, chopped up and added to three tablespoons of boiling water. It is the juice you want, not the leaves. Allow the water to cool before adding it to the melted soap. Then simply add all other ingredients before pouring into the moulds.

Lemon and Chamomile Shampoo Bar

This is for blonde hair, gives a great shine and is good for the scalp.

You Will Need:

200g (6½ oz) glycerine soap
20ml (4 tbsps) chamomile infusion juice
10ml (2 tbsps) lemon juice

The infusion is made with two chamomile teabags added to just enough boiling water to cover them. Allow the liquid to cool and then press them out. Add the lemon juice to the infusion and then add this to the soap. Pour into the moulds.

Lice Repellent Shampoo Bar

This is a strong shampoo bar that helps to keep lice at bay, although it is not completely guaranteed. Well, it worked for us when we were teachers.

You Will Need:

200g (6½ oz) glycerine soap
12 drops of tea tree oil

Melt the soap and then add the tea tree oil. This is then allowed to set into a single big bar.

Big Fat Scrubber

This is a great scrub and a good one for the shower, but don't use it on your soft bits!

You Will Need:

200g (6½ oz) glycerine soap
10g (⅓ oz) salt
10ml (2 tbsps) almond oil
40g (½ oz) ground almonds

Simply melt the soap and add the ingredients, the salt first, then the oil and finally the ground almonds. Set it in a big bar because you will always be dropping it. It has a lot of salt to make it hard, but the shower water simply washes this away. You can set a rope in it if you really feel you must.

Shower Gel

This is easy to make and is especially useful if you have skin problems because there isn't much soap in it.

You Will Need:

200g (6½ oz) glycerine soap
25g (½ oz) salt (You can omit this if you like, it acts to thicken the liquid)
10ml (2 tbsps) almond, olive, or any favourites oil
550ml (1 pint) boiling water

Simply melt the soap and carefully add the hot water, stirring slowly all the time. Add the remaining ingredients. Allow it to cool and store for use. You can add colours if you like from the kitchen cupboard, but not too harshly; you don't want a painted skin.

Child's Soap

Yes, you guessed it! Glycerine soap is so mild in action that it is used neat to make soap specifically for children. You can add a few drops of oil to the mixture if you wish. For young children the fewer harsh chemicals you use on them, the better, so keep it simple. Experiment with 5% of baby oil as a starting point.

T-Gel Soap

In the UK there is an excellent product called T-Gel, and doubtless it has its equivalent counterparts around the world. It is a coal tar based soap and has been excellent for our own son's psoriasis. When we started making our own soap we hit on the idea of making a bar of T-Gel soap which consists of 200g glycerine soap and 30g (a little over 15% of the total weight) of T-Gel along with

20g of salt to thicken the bar. This has worked wonders for his skin. But please don't take this a guarantee of success; it might not work for all types of skin problem, but it is worth a try.

Shaving Soap

This started as something of a joke. I wondered what would happen if you combined soap with aftershave. Well, you get smelly soap. But the old fashioned lather soap is simply made by adding almond oil to glycerine soap at a rate of 15%. It is rather oily but it gives a good and well lubricated surface to shave against, and it soothes the skin as well as moisturising it.

Disinfectant Soap

Regardless of how you make your soap, either from lye or otherwise, you can make disinfectant soap quite easily. Simply add some bought disinfectant to your mixture at a level of 1%. If you use a standard fragranced disinfectant, make sure you only add 1 drop for every 100g of soap. This will be mild enough. Carbolic soap was good at killing germs but it was never kind to the skin. Modern disinfectants contain tryclosan, yet another man made chemical. You can add five drops of TCP to your 100g of soap if you like the smell and this product will also make for a brilliant disinfectant. A combination of 5g of salt and 25g (1oz) of vinegar to 200g of soap also makes for a good, if slightly smelly, disinfecting soap.

A WARNING. Do not use untried chemicals on skin; you might be allergic to them. In all the following recipes use a very diluted solution first to test yourself. Also make sure, should you choose to set up a still like the one referred to, that you can any kind of accidents in the home.

Precycle!

Making Ointments and Balms

Ointments are the method by which we add active ingredients to our skin. If you can get hold of lanolin, use it. It is even worth buying wool fleeces to boil off the lanolin. You will need a big pan to boil a fleece. Keep the boiling going for an hour, by which time you should see a yellowish oil in the water. Add a handful of salt. Boil this liquid until the water has nearly all gone. The final wax, on cooling, can be purified by shaking it with a mixture of olive oil and water.

The Basic Ointment

Use 100g (3½oz) of lanolin, olive oil, or lard. (lard is often considered the best!) and melt this with 25g (1oz) of beeswax. Add to this 25g (1oz) of your water as prepared above, or 6 drops of essential oil. Use a water bath to melt your materials and you can pour the wax into moulds, tins or bottles. You will have to experiment in order to get the consistency you require but you can reheat the ointment in order to start again if not initially successful.

Making Waters

The mainstay of personal grooming for many centuries was rose water. This method is just as good for other flowers from the garden such as lavender.

You will need to set up a still and boil the petals or flowers into a second pot. The way you do this is to get a large old pot and place a brick inside it, or anything to make a shelf. You are going to fill the pot with water and place a receptacle such as a jam jar on the shelf. The pan you use will need to have a lid that will allow you to turn it upside down.

The still comes into its own when you put crushed ice on the upturned lid. When you set the pan to boil, fragrance laden steam will condense on the lid and drip into the jar on the shelf. Empty the jar into a bottle every fifteen minutes, checking the fragrance. When the quality of the water has reduced, replenish the flowers or petals.

Rose water is a great toner and lavender a good antiseptic, leaving the skin feeling fresh and clean. You can make all kinds of oiled water in this way. It doesn't take long and is great fun, as well as being really useful.

Chamomile

This is a brilliant concoction to make for its general soothing antiseptic qualities. You can use this to sooth nappy rash as well as to clean sensitive skin. It is also considered a very safe herb to use. Simply take a combination of leaves and flowers and distil them as above.

Fennel

This is good at removing wrinkles, especially when combined with Lady's Mantle, which make for an excellent combination. Simply collect a few leaves of Lady's Mantle and add them to the boiling with a chopped fennel bulb.

There is a recipe for fennel/Lady's Mantle vinegar for the face. Put equal quantities by weight into a jar of vinegar and leave it to steep for several weeks. Then strain out the plant material and dilute the vinegar with ten times the amount of water. Use raspberry vinegar for a nicer aroma. This solution's mild astringency is said to deal effectively with wrinkles.

Precycle!

Lady's Mantle

This is anti-bacterial and makes a great wash for damaged skin. You can also use it to help with bleeding gums. The plant can be distilled as above and the liquid cooled and kept in a dark bottle. It is not poisonous and can be swallowed. It has been used as a tonic and an appetite restorer for many centuries.

Lavender

The word lavender comes from the Latin 'lavare' which means to wash. It was taken round the world by the Romans and has been used for washing ever since. It is nicely scented, but also has antibiotic properties. More importantly still, it acts as an insect repellent, the very best thing for working outdoors.

Lemon Balm

This is a soothing plant that has been used to help people sleep. However, it has been discovered to have anti-viral properties and is very good as a lip balm. Use it as an ointment as above by adding 25ml (1oz) to the mix. There have been some studies about using this balm with cold sores that suggests it reduces both the swelling and redness. Of course, this makes a brilliant balm for winter lips, particularly if you use olive oil and beeswax. Improve the flavour with some raspberry oil and a little honey.

Red Clover

This plant is used to treat skin conditions. If you want to be really clever you could say to people that clover is full of phyto-estrogens and exerts a protective element for the cardiovascular system in women during the menopause. A wash of red clover flower water will help with spots and other problems such as eczema.

Rose

Roses are special for the skin, providing all kinds of wonderful elements. Rose water is lovely to wash in and makes you feel calm. It makes a wonderful eye wash and is the best wash by far for night-time use. Your own fragrant roses will be fine to use, but you can make a bath of rosewater and rosehip boiled together which, by the way, is also full of vitamin C.

Sage

Sage water is astringent, tightening the skin and pores and thus temporarily reducing lines. It is an antioxidant and is antiseptic too. In fact it is the ideal wash after a day in the garden. If you have sweated heavily, this wash will help prevent outbreaks of spots. It is also useful applied to stings and bites, and you can even rub a leaf on a bite.

Thyme

This is a wonderful deodorizer and has fantastic cleaning properties, as well as relieving irritation. It has an antioxidant property and is used in many very expensive anti-aging creams. It protects against insects and, in particular, scabies.

Raspberry

This water makes for a good antiseptic for the eyes and other delicate personal zones because it is mild in action but also very soothing.

Precycle!

Calendula

The common pot marigold has many completely natura
uses. Firstly as an antiseptic with a difference. If you can
get the essential oil, all well and good, but if not you can
use the leaves of the plant. There are so many uses for
it that we are going to look in detail at two right away;
toothpaste and deodorant.

Calendula Deodorant

The basic action of an under-arm deodorant is to kill the
bacteria that cause smells in the first place. Everyday
washing, particularly with good soap, and maintaining a
comfortable ambient temperature should be more than
enough to keep BO at bay. However, working in of-
fices rather than outdoors often creates an environment
where armpits get a little out of control.

You can buy calendula oil online and from health shops
and you can use its to make deodorant. But you can
also make water with it as described above. It can be
used for all kinds of skin problems like nappy rash, but is
best used as a deodorant because of its anti-bacterial and
anti- fungal nature. You can make the deodorant by adding 25ml (1oz) to the cream recipe and simply smear a
little on the underarm. You can combine both calendula
and lavender for a slightly more fragrant version.

Toothpaste

You can make the best toothpaste for just pennies by
using baking powder. Make a concoction of calendula
as above and use it to create a paste with the baking
powder. Simply put an amount of baking powder into a
bowl and use the liquid diluted 50:50 with boiled water.
Work the powder into a paste and add a few drops of

peppermint oil. Alternatively, you can make a concoction as above using mint leaves and use this to create the toothpaste. The baking powder has a cleaning effect in its own right and is mild enough to use on your teeth. You can, if you like, add a couple of crushed fluoride tablets to the mix. In this way you will have as good a toothpaste as you can buy in the shops, but for pennies.

This toothpaste will keep indefinitely in a plastic pot with an airtight lid. Some recipes call for the use of hydrogen peroxide, but I feel this is a dangerous move because too strong a solution could cause problems.

Mouthwash

Millions of pounds are spent annually on all sorts of mouthwashes. The main point here is that they have to freshen the breath, promote healing and have some antiseptic properties.

Rosemary and Mint Mouthwash

Mix equal quantities of mint leaves, anise seeds and rosemary leaves; about 5g (¼ oz) of each into half a litre (1 pint) of boiling water and infuse for about 15-20 minutes. Strain, cool it and use it as a mouthwash to gargle with.

Baking Soda and Tea Tree Mouthwash

Add 2 drops of mint oil, 1 drop of tea tree and 5g (1 level teaspoon) of baking powder to a cup of water. This will keep in a bottle and tastes nicely minty.

Precycle!

Lemon Mouthwash

Dilute the juice of a lemon into a cup of water together with a tablespoon of aloe vera juice and a teaspoon of baking powder. The baking powder neutralises the acid in the lemon and this makes for a really healing mouth-wash that is very pleasant to use.

Hair Treats

There are so many expensive hair treatments on the market that you could spend a fortune, but before you do, have a go at some of these ideas for healthy, shiny hair.

This is a recipe for home made shampoo that is very mild and is suitable for any hair type. It needs to be kept in the fridge and will store for 7-10 days as it doesn't contain any preservatives. The following recipe provides 5-7 applications, so it won't be wasted if you either wash your hair often or it is used by two to three people. It uses soapwort, so called because it has the same effect as soap and has traditionally been used to wash the hair and body. Soapwort root can be purchased from herbalists and health shops.

Soapwort Shampoo

You Will Need:

250ml (½ pint) water
1½ tbsps dried soapwort root
the juice of ½ a lemon

Bring the water to the boil and add the soapwort. Cover and simmer gently for 20 minutes. Remove from the heat and add the lemon juice. Allow the mixture to cool thoroughly before pouring it into a clean bottle or jar. Use it exactly as a shop bought shampoo.

If you don't have time to wash your hair but want to freshen it up, cut a lime into thin slices, remove the pips and rub it over the scalp. Then comb your hair and leave.

Hair Rinses

These are ideal as light conditioning treatments or for using after conditioning to add shine. They are very easy to prepare and can make all the difference to how healthy your hair looks.

The first ones use vinegar which is excellent for smoothing the cuticle of the hair and promoting shine. Don't worry about the smell. It may linger whilst the hair is drying, but once the hair is dry it will have gone. Also, don't rinse these out. Leave them in place to get the benefit of the ingredients.

Add 1 tablespoon of cider vinegar and the juice of 1 lemon to a pint of tepid water to enhance the shine of all hair types. The same can be done with malt vinegar for dry or treated hair and red wine vinegar enhances the shine of auburn hair.

Beer makes an excellent hair rinse too, but it does leave the hair a bit smelly, although it gives fine hair body and shine. Simply pour 100ml (4oz) of beer into a jug with 250ml (¾ pint) water and use as the final rinse.

Herbal hair rinses are excellent for healthy hair. When you have poured the rinse through the hair, massage them into your scalp using your fingertips and towel dry, leaving them in the hair to get the full benefit.

Precycle!

Rosemary is excellent for dark brown hair. It enhances the colour and shine and smells very clean. Add two tablespoons of chopped fresh rosemary to ¾ pint of boiling water and stir and macerate the leaves. Allow it to cool before applying on the hair.

Chamomile has been traditionally used on fair hair. It adds highlights and shine to blondes. Steep 3 chamomile tea bags in boiling water and allow it to cool before using. You may also put a handful of fresh or dried flowers in ½ pint of boiling water. Allowit to cool, then strain before using. The lightening effect is further enhanced if you add the juice of a lemon to the cooled mixture.

Thyme leaves steeped in the same way will help with an itchy scalp. It is soothing and helps to counteract dandruff.

Hair Conditioners and Moisturisers

A tablespoon of pure coconut oil is an excellent hair conditioner, which helps with dryness and leaves the hair soft and shiny. Simply apply it to dry hair and leave it on for as long as you can. Shampoo it out and use one of the above rinses to finish the hair.

Banana Conditioner

Mash 1 large banana and mix it in with 1 tablespoon of honey. Add 2 tablespoons of natural yogurt and stir well. Apply to damp hair, put on a plastic shower cap and wrap a warm towel around the head. Leave this on for an hour before shampooing out.

Avocado Hair Mask

Mash an avocado and add an egg yolk. Apply this to dry hair and leave for 30 minutes. Massage it into your hair before shampooing out.

Mayo Mask

Add 1 tablespoon of olive oil to 2 tablespoons of mayonnaise. Apply this to dry hair and cover with a shower cap. Leave it on for 20 minutes before shampooing out.

Lice Problems

Head lice areactually very common in children, but can be deterred by using tea tree oil in soap. In the soap making section you will find a shampoo bar that deters them. This don't kill the lice, but they do get off pretty quickly because they don't like the smell. A final rinse of the hair in calendula concoction also helps.

An old fashioned remedy for treating an infestation is to comb out as many as you can with a nit comb and then wash the hair in tea tree. You can use ordinary shampoo with four or five drops of tea tree in your hand. Leave this on to dry and then wash it out. The next day comb again and then apply a liberal amount of olive oil and rub it in well. This clogs the lice's air holes and they die. A further wash with tea tree laden shampoo and a good comb will help too. Repeat this after two days and again after another two days. This gives the eggs a chance to hatch and you can then kill off any young.

There are some homemade recipes for insecticides, but it is illegal to make them and for good reason. If you boil up marigold flowers and leaves and allow the liquid to evaporate, you will get a concentrated solution of pyrethrums, but you will have very little control over both its strength and the effect on the intended target. In this case the law is there to protect you. Some websites also say to apply Listerine to the head, but please don't! If all else fails, go to see your doctor!

All Hail Aloe Vera

Everyone interested in self-sufficiency should grow aloes. It is a miracle plant that has so many uses in the home. It is comparatively easy to grow and is available from any garden centre. Simply place the plant in a large pot indoors near a sunny window. A sunny greenhouse would be ideal. In the winter allow the soil to dry out before watering again and, in the spring, give it a liberal feed with liquid fertiliser over a period of a month. Pot it on at the beginning of the summer. You can increase your stock by cutting off the side branches that appear and potting them in moist compost.

Use the gel in the leaves to treat burns, stings and dilute it to make drinks or facial cleansers and for applying to all kinds of skin eruptions. It is extremely effective when diluted by at least three times the amount of boiled water and allowed to cool.

Burns can be dealt with by removing a lower leaf and simply squeezing the gel out onto the burn. Don't forget that if a burn is greater than 3cm in diameter it should receive medical attention.

Cleansing

If you have dry skin massage coconut oil and a drop of lavender oil into the skin, then clean it off with a warm face cloth. This will remove dirt and facial make-up and leaves skin both soft and clean. I would recommend using ½ a teaspoon of coconut oil to 2 drops of lavender oil.

A really good recipe for home made cleanser which is

particularly effective on normal skin is the following:

You Will Need:

2 tbsps cornflour
2 tbsps glycerine
70ml (2½fl oz) water

Cook all the ingredients gently in a pan until the mixture becomes transparent. Allow it to cool slightly, pour it into a sterilised glass jar and seal Use it when cool by spreading a little of the mixture over the face and then remove it with a tissue.

To vary the recipe add a little essential oil to the mixture after cooking, but check which essential oil is most suitable for your skin type.

Essential Oils					
Skin Type	Lavender	Tea Tree	Chamomile	Geranium	Rose
Oily	✓	✓			
Sensitive	✓		✓		
Dry	✓		✓		✓
Troubled		✓	✓	✓	
Anti-ageing	✓				✓
De-congesting		✓		✓	

When using essential oils always remember to follow the dilution ratio, which is 1 drop of essential oil to a minimum of 5ml of carrier oil or liquid. NEVER put the oil directly onto the skin without diluting it first.

A soothing cleanser for mildly irritated skin is made by

using equal amounts of sweet almond oil and aloe vera gel. It will need a good shaking in a plastic or glass container, as it is difficult to combine the two ingredients. Use it as soon as it is mixed by spreading it over the face and gently massaging it in with the fingertips. Remove it with a warm face cloth or tissues.

Toning

After cleansing, a toning rinse with cool water is sometimes sufficient to refresh the skin, but an added boost to this simple idea is to put some mineral water in a small pump action bottle and to keep it in the fridge till needed. It can then be used to spritz the face. My all-time favourite toning spritz uses honey and water

Honey Water Toner

You Will Need:

50ml (2fl oz) boiled water
1 tbsp clear honey

Add the honey to the hot water and leave them to cool. Pour into a spray bottle and store in fridge ready for action. Spray it over the face after cleansing and see how soft your skin feels.

Lavender and Rosemary Toning Water

The combination of lavender and rosemary makes a very soothing toning lotion for all skin types.

You Will Need:

10 lavender flower heads
15g (1/2 oz) fresh or 10g (1/3 oz) dried rosemary
200ml (6fl oz) boiling water

Pour the water over the lavender and rosemary and leave to cool, stirring the mixture occasionally. Strain into a sterilised bottle and store in the fridge. Use regularly after cleansing to tone the skin. This mixture will keep well for 2 weeks if stored in the fridge.

Witch Hazel

For a super clean feeling, distilled witch hazel in a little cooled, boiled water makes an excellent toner for normal to oily skin.

You Will Need:

20ml (4 tbsps) distilled witch hazel
10ml (2 tbsps) cooled boiled water
3 drops lavender essential oil

Mix all the ingredients together in a bottle and apply to skin with a cotton wool pad. For troubled or very oily skin use tea tree oil in place of lavender and use 30ml (6tbsps) of witch hazel.

Cider Vinegar

In cooled boiled water this makes an excellent toner for normal skin.

You Will Need:

30ml (6tbsps) boiled water
4 tsps cider vinegar

Mix and use this as with the witch hazel recipe.

Precycle!

Coconut Milk

Powdered coconut milk mixed in warm water will soothe tight, dry skin.

You Will Need:

10ml (2 tbsps) powdered coconut milk
150ml (5fl oz) boiled water, cooled slightly

Mix the coconut powder with the hot water thoroughly. I use a small whisk for this as you don't want any lumps in the mixture when applying it to your face. It is best applied with cotton wool pads and pressed onto the skin rather than rubbed.

Face masks

The point of a face mask is to hydrate the skin and deal with minor infections that we normally wouldn't even notice. It is silly to imagine that a face mask gives any form of nutrition to the skin because it is applied to a dead layer. All the mask can do is to deal with any invading fungal and bacterial infestations of the scales, plump up the dead scales, remove excess scales and ensure that the pores are free and unblocked.

Banana Face Mask

You Will Need:

1 egg yolk
6-8 drops sweet almond oil
1 ripe mashed banana
1 tsp lemon juice

Mix all the ingredients together in a bowl and apply to the face, avoiding both the eyes and lips. Leave it for 20 minutes and remove with a tissue and finish off with a refreshing splash of cool water and a toner of your choice.

Honey Mask

This mask seems to help tighten the skin, and so evens out the complexion. If your skin is feeling a little saggy then this is the one to try.

You Will Need:

1 egg white
2 tbsps honey
1 tbsp finely ground oatmeal

Mix the ingredients to a thick paste and apply to the face. Leave it to dry and then rinse off with cool water.

Clean and Soft Mask

The fruit acids in apple help to exfoliate and brighten the skin, so use this when your face is feeling or looking a little tired or dull.

You Will Need:

1 whole egg
1 tbsp clear honey
1 mashed apple
1 tbsp ground oatmeal

Combine the egg and oatmeal and mix in the honey. Add the mashed apple and apply to the face. Leave for 20 mins and rinse off with cool water.

Precycle!

Avocado Softener

For very dry complexions there is nothing better than an avocado for cleansing and putting both oils and moisture back into the skin.

You Will Need:

1 mashed avocado
1 egg yolk
2 tsps olive oil

Combine all the ingredients in a bowl and apply to the face. Leave on for as long as you can stand it but for at least 20 minutes. Rinse off with cool water.

Toning Mask

For a toning treatment, cucumber is an excellent ingredient as it is gentle on the skin but has a good toning effect.

You Will Need:

1 tbsp powdered milk
1/3 of a cucumber, mashed
2 tbsps natural yogurt

Mash the cucumber and the powdered milk together in a bowl and add the yogurt. Stir it well and apply to the face. Leave for 20 minutes before rinsing off with cool water.

Facial Scrubs

Using a facial scrub once or twice a week will help to keep the skin looking healthy, and there are probably many items already in your cupboards that will work effectively as a face exfoliant.

Hair and Beauty

The best way to prepare the skin is to place a fairly warm face cloth over your face for a few seconds just as the old fashioned barbers used to do when they were giving a gentleman a close shave. This opens up the pores, ready to be cleaned out with your choice of treatment.

The first recipe is the one I use most and is also the first I ever made. You have to use this over the sink as it does get messy, but it is worth it for softer, brighter skin.

Oatmeal, Milk and Lavender Scrub

You Will Need:

30g (1oz) medium oatmeal
1 tbsp dried milk powder
6 drops lavender essential oil
30ml (6tbsps) cooled, boiled water

Mix the water and milk powder to a smooth, thin paste. Add the oats and the lavender oil and stir well. Apply to the face and massage in circular movements, taking care to avoid the eyes, but it is gentle enough to use over the lips and actually seems to stimulate the circulation and so makes them look fuller. Massage each area of the face for 30-40 seconds, then rinse off with cool water.

If you have a tendency to suffer from the odd spot, then add 2-3 drops of tea tree oil as well as the lavender and pay particular attention to the spot area when massaging with the scrub.

The following almond scrub is particularly good for keeping the skin looking healthy and cleansing the pores. Geranium oil is very good for decongesting the pores and getting rid of any blackheads.

Almond Scrub

You Will Need:

20g (³/₄ oz) ground almonds
2 tsps sweet almond oil
5 drops geranium essential oil

Combine the ingredients together and use as with the previous scrub, working on all the areas that need most attention, principally the nose, around the mouth and the chin.

A combination of coconut oil and ground almonds really cleans the skin thoroughly and gets the pores deeply clean. You may add a little essential oil to the following recipe to help your skin type if you wish, but it is very effective without. Your skin will be left clean and very soft after this treatment.

Coconut and Almond Scrub

You Will Need:

15g (¹/₂ oz) ground almonds
10g (¹/₃ oz) desiccated coconut
1 level tbsp coconut oil

Put the coconut oil in a warm bowl where it will melt straight away. Add the other ingredients, mixing well and massage it over the face with circular movements. Continue this for at least 60 seconds, but no longer than 2 minutes. Rinse well with warm water and finish off with a toner to close the pores.

Sugar Scrub

A really strong facial scrub that is good for dull and

flaky skin but which still needs something gentle. This uses sugar as the exfoliant. Use caster sugar because the rough grains of granulated sugar might be just too rough.

You Will Need:

25g (1oz approx.) of caster sugar
1 tbsp olive oil

Combine the two ingredients together and massage over the face in circular movements. Continue this for 30 seconds or until the skin feels tingly, then rinse it off completely with warm water. This can make the skin feel a little oily afterwards. You can use a mild glycerine soap to remove this.

Moisturisers

Making a home made moisturiser is a little more complicated, but is still worthwhile. Always remember that if you are storing your cream, do make sure it is in a sterilised air tight container.

Rich Moisture Cream

The next recipe is for a rich moisturising cream and uses beeswax, which you can get from your local bee society. Pure rose oil is very expensive but gives a luxurious finish to the cream and is particularly good as an anti-ageing ingredient.

You Will Need:

5g (1/4 oz) beeswax
50ml (2fl oz) almond oil
10 drops of rose essential oil

Melt the beeswax over a low heat until it is completely liquid. Add the almond oil and the rose oil and pour into sterilised jars. Seal them well and use within 2 months.

Light Moisturiser

For a lighter moisturiser, the following uses glycerine to give a more fluid lotion.

You Will Need:

20g (³/₄ oz) coconut oil
20ml (4 tbsps) glycerine
8 drops of chamomile essential oil

Melt the coconut oil in a warm bowl and stir in the glycerine and chamomile oil. Pour into sterile jars and seal well. Use it within 2 months.

Hand Treatments

Sugar Hand Scrub

Mix 1 tablespoon of olive oil with 1 teaspoon of sugar and apply to the hands. Gently massage this into the skin in circular movements. Continue this for a few minutes or until you feel your hands tingling as your circulation is stimulated. Place your hands in warm water for a few seconds whilst continuing to massage them, then rinse the sugar off with cool water and pat dry.

My friend's remedy for dry hands is to massage a little sunflower oil into them, then put on her rubber gloves and wash up. This does make scientific sense. The hot water used for washing up helps the oil to sink deeper into the hands and leaves them very soft. If they feel too oily after removing your gloves, rinse them in warm water and dry.

I do a lot of gardening and find it very difficult to get my nails clean afterwards. An excellent tip to prevent this is to scrape your nails along a bar of soap, trapping a little of the soap under your nails. This stops the dirt from getting trapped under them and allows any that does accumulate to be washed away easily afterwards.

To stimulate blood flow to the nails rub some almond oil mixed with a few drops of lavender essential oil into the cuticles whilst watching television or listening to the radio. This is great for softening the cuticles and keeping the nails naturally pink.

Nail Strengthening Soak

If you have soft nails as I have, this really helps to strengthen them without drying them out. Simply soak your hands in a bowl containing ½ a pint of warm water and 2 tablespoons of cider vinegar. Leave them to soak for 5-10 minutes, then pat dry and massage a little sweet almond oil into both the nails and cuticles.

Hand Smoothing Mask

Mix 1 tablespoon of coconut milk powder with 3 tablespoons of hot water and stir until dissolved. Add 2 level tablespoons of oatmeal and mix to a thick paste, adding a little more oatmeal if it isn't thick enough. Apply to the hands and leave to dry. This is a lovely way to relax for 20-30 minutes as you cannot do much with your hands except rest them on a towel and perhaps listen to some soothing music. Finally, rinse off in warm water and you will notice how soft your hands feel.

Precycle!

Fit Feet

Feet take a hammering in our busy lives, so looking after them is essential and we often forget how good a little foot pampering can feel. Something as simple as a foot soak can make all the difference to how we feel.

Soothing Foot Balm

For a really soothing foot balm, mix 1 teaspoon of cider vinegar into a small pot of natural yogurt and massage this over your feet. Leave it for 10 miutes, then rinse them off with warm water.

Foot Soak

Stir 2 tablespoons of epsom salts in warm water and soak your feet for 15 minutes. Add lavender oil to relax or eucalyptus oil to revive. To freshen your feet in hot weather add a few drops of peppermint oil to your cool footbath and pat dry.

Rub sea salt into your feet before soaking in a warm footbath containing neroli oil(if you can find it). If not then add a few drops of geranium oil instead.

In Winter, when feet are cold and tired, an old fash-ioned mustard footbath really helps. Mix 3 teaspoons of mustard powder with a little water to make a smooth paste. Add this to a bowl of water that is warmer than your body temperature and soak your feet for a good 10 minutes at least.

To keep your feet feeling clean and healthy soak them in cool water containing tea tree oil for about 15 minutes. After soaking, rub a teaspoon of coconut oil into your feet and wrap them in a warm towel. They will feel soft and incredibly comfortable.

Vitamins and Supplements

Pick-me-ups and Tonics

This section is intended to show that you can get all the vitamins and supplements you need from either the garden or the wild. It is not, however, a treatise on herbal medicine. If you are ill the best advice you can get is to go and seek out your doctor. It is, however, intended as a way of showing you how to replace many of those pills and supplements we all buy in the shops.

Vitamin C

It seems that mankind somehow lost the ability to make vitamin C a few hundred thousand years ago when a mysterious mutation took place in the population. Quite how this mutation became so dominant in the population isn't known, but thankfully the vitamin is a very common molecule and, since we get a reasonable amount from our daily food intake, we have no real problem. However, research has shown that mammals who do make their own vitamin C do so in huge quantities. A rat, for example, makes several grams a day,which is many hundred times our recommended daily allowance,

Precycle!

yet its body weight is a tiny fraction of ours. Vitamin C is without doubt a really important molecule and it does a lot for both our general health and our ability to fight disease.

Rosehips are nature's single best source of vitamin C and a spoonful of this a day is quite enough for your recommended daily allowance and tastes wonderful too. It is very easy to make.

You Will Need:

2 litres (4 pints approx.) water
1 kg (2.2lbs) rosehips
500g (1lb) sugar

Mash all the rosehips and add them to a pan with ¾ of your water. Bring this to the boil and simmer for 15 minutes. Carefully strain the pulp, keeping the liquid in a second pan. Boil the rest of your water and give the strained pulp a second soaking for 15 minutes, straining again and keeping the pulp. Reduce the pulp until you have about 500ml (1pint) and bring it to a vigorous boil while you add the sugar. When all the sugar has dissolved, allow the solution to cool and then decant it into sterile bottles. It should keep all year, but you will have to make several batches of these quantities if it is to last a whole family for a year. It is also brilliant for getting any slow fermenting wine off to a flying start.

Teas for Health

Elsewhere in this book we have written about herbal teas as something good to drink. They have long been used for medical reasons and the following table shows a wide variety of their uses as supplements.

Herb	Part Used	Benefits	Notes
Celery	Seeds or leaf	Digestion problems are soothed by this tea	
Chamomile	Flowers and leaves	Tension and tummy ache	Do not suck the leaves raw, they can cause blisters
Fennel	Seed and leaf	Digestive problems	Aniseed flavour
Lemon balm	Leaf	Soothing relaxant for the anxious	
Marigold	Flower	Anti bacterial	Antiseptic of yesteryear
Mint	Leaf	Wonderful for the digestion	Completely safe
Nettle	Leaf	Detoxification and general pick me up	
Rosemary	Leaf	Antiseptic and pain relief	Can increase blood pressure
Rose	Petal	Calming	
Sage	Leaf	Antiseptic and excellent astringent	Do not use in pregnancy

Precycle!

Sage has been cultivated all over the world since the earliest days of farming, some ten thousand years ago. It has been found in the pyramids and in other ancient burials sites and is contained in just about every herbal text that has ever been written. The scientific name, *salvia officinalis,* means official saver, or official cleanser. The Romans revered this herb and a special ceremony was followed each year before it was harvested. In my childhood we used to put germaline on all our cuts and today there are a vast range of things in tubes designed to do just the same. For the previous hundred generations of humankind, sage did the job just as well.

There is a North South divide when it comes to using sage in the kitchen. In Spain, Italy and France the herb tends to be used to flavour sauces. It is rarely used to flavour meat directly, except in Roman sausages. It is used in Germany and the UK to directly flavour and preserve both sausages and other meats and this is a direct consequence of the weather. The chance of air drying a sausage, or any other meat for that matter, is significantly reduced in the cold, wet north, so sage was added to the mixes with a good deal of extra salt.

Sage is ideal as a mild antiseptic and a little chopped up in yoghurt makes an excellent salve, especially for minor abrasions, or a teaspoonful boiled in a cup of water and allowed to cool is an excellent treatment for small burns and mouth problems, from ulcers to cold sores.

Other Pharmaceuticals

The word "pharmaceutical" simply means "plant medicine" and the pharma part of the word also appears in the word farming. Nearly all of our modern drugs originate from the plant kingdom in one form or another. The earliest medical text books were called herbals. Modern medicine has taken the active ingredients from a whole world of plants and isolated them, manufacturing them so that doctors can treat you with the exact chemical in precisely the right quantity to make you well. But there are some chemicals that have proven to be really beneficial that we can all take regularly to keep us in continuing good health.

The Famous Five

Garlic

Garlic, in one of its many forms, is grown all over the world and has been cultivated for its flavour since Neolithic times. It is written about in ancient Indian writings but the use of this amazing vegetable probably predates writing itself.

The plant that we would all recognise as garlic is not found in the wild, but there are numerous members of the same genus. Alliums are one of the few members of the lily family that are not actually poisonous.

It did not take long for mankind to realise the health benefits of garlic, especially its use as a preservative for meats and cheese and that rubbing it on cuts stopped infections. Of course, the medical claims for this vegetable are many and varied and properly conducted 'double blind' medical research has found that the health benefits of using garlic are well founded.

During the Great War the government paid farmers a shilling a punnet for garlic bulbs. These were crushed into a paste and smeared onto field dressings to act as an antiseptic. It is estimated that millions of soldiers owed their lives to this plant.

The regular use of garlic is good for the digestion and removing or fighting intestinal parasites. It clears away

Precycle!

harmful bacteria while allowing beneficial bacteria to grow unadulterated. It has an anti-bacterial, anti-fungal and anti-viral action, but has also been shown to reduce blood pressure, make the heart healthier and 'un-harden' (to some extent, at least) hardened arteries. (None of these factors make garlic a self treatment for high blood pressure or poor circulatory problems, but as a well known British supermarket says, "Every Little Helps!")

You should try to consume at least a clove a day, grated or macerated in some food or other. Cooking garlic actually increases its efficacy, so plan to get garlic into your cooking.

Honey

Honey is a wonderful substance because it has to keep pure and without infection in the hive all year round. Bees use it for both energy for their immune system. We can benefit from its curative properties too. Honey contains enzymes and preserving chemicals derived from plants that the bees have visited. It is antiseptic and antibiotic to a remarkable degree. The sugars in honey are the easiest to metabolise and they actively promote growth. Honey is now being used to help flesh grow and in the treatment of ulcers. It also has a wonderful action on the back of the throat if you have an infection but, more than anything else, it makes you smile.

Propolis is a bee glue used in the hive to glue anything up. It has strong antiseptic properties. If an animal dies, say a mouse, which is quite frequent inside the hive, the bees will glue it up in propolis to stop the mouse from rotting and causing infection in the hive. Propolis is also used to glue the parts of the hive together. This substance has wonderful healing properties and it is said that beekeepers live to a great age because they chew it.

Honey contains pollen and hayfever is caused by pollen. If you regularly take locally produced honey you will be taking in small amounts of the local pollen. This will not cause symptoms but will immunise you against any trouble later in the year. It is not 100% effective, but does help considerably.

Honey Health Drink

You Will Need:

2 tbsps honey
2 drops propolis
the juice of a lemon
250ml (8fl oz) freshly squeezed orange juice

Warm a tablespoon in boiling water and use it to spoon the honey into a mug or glass. Add the propolis and lemon juice and stir vigorously. Heat the orange juice in a pan to body temperature and pour it over the honey mixture. Stir well and drink it straight away.

This really helps if you have a sore throat or a cold coming on. Honey is known for its anti-viral properties and the propolis is both soothing and anti-septic.

Both locally sourced honey and propolis can be purchased from beekeeping associations in your area.

Apple

"An apple a day keeps the doctor away" is very true! There are so many benefits in apples that everyone should drink a glass of their own apple juice every day. Don't bother to buy apple juice, just apples, and juice them yourself.

Apples are very beneficial to health. The flavanoid phlo-

Precycle!

ridzin, found only in apples, can help women suffering from osteoporosis. A study shows that children with asthma who drank apple juice on a daily basis suffered less from wheezing. Quercetin in apples is also believed to protect the brain cells from free radical damage that may lead to Alzheimer's disease. Pectin in apples lowers cholesterol and the daily consumption of apples can reduce cholesterol considerably. And apples have also been cited as helping prevent lung, colon, liver and breast cancer.

Tomatoes

Follow our recipe for tomato sauce, passata and other tomato products because they are especially health promoting. Young boys should have the equivalent of a tablespoon a day because the lycopene not only helps the development of their genitals, it also protects them and other glandular parts of the body from cancers.

Lycopene is really amazing at protecting from cancers and should be taken on a regular basis by everyone. No wonder the tomato was called the love apple, because it certainly loves our delicate bits.

Dandelion

This plant's scientific name is *taraxacum officinale*, which means the official cure for disorders. It is particularly good at helping with urinary disorders, though it cannot be stressed enough the importance of seeking medical advice should you have any ongoing problems.

Dandelion is full of carotene, beta-carotene being a precursor to vitamin A and the trace elements in the plant make it the most important vegetable to take for an all round dose of vitamins and minerals. It is best taken as a salad vegetable when the leaves are young, but they can be used in exactly the same way as spinach. The sodium content is also ideal for use in a salt-free diet, being present in just the right amount.

Precycle!

Resources

The Importance of Good Pans and Lots of Bottles and Jars

Given the chance the average family would probably throw away hundreds of bottles and jars a year or, at best, recycle them. The value of a good screw top bottle cannot be overestimated for storing sauces, drinks, preserves and any short lived material. If you buy screw top bottles, let us say a sauce bottle, the lid will have a rubber seal inside it. This seal keeps it airtight and so helps to keep the contents from spoiling. These kind of bottles can be used again and again for materials meant to last more than a month, but only use them once for short lived items; find a different use for them next time. This is because the seal wears out, especially if you expose it to boiling water and cleaning chemicals.

Bottles with a 'metalised' plastic cover across the open-

Precycle!

ing are no good for storing long term, but you can find short term uses for them. You should also buy new bottles for storage. "Kilner" type jars are about the best. You can get these in all sizes and they are ideal for everything from jam to pickles. Make sure you get a liberal supply of spare rubber seals too, for the same reasons.

Plastic lemonade bottles are great for beer, wine and other drinks. If you buy cheap lemonade in large bottles they come already sterile so you can pour out the contents into jars for immediate use and refill them straight away with your product. This way you save a job and at the same time save the planet from the harshness of the sterilising process.

Until recently the most used piece of equipment in the modern kitchen was the can opener. This tool has been rendered obsolete, not by better cooking with fresh ingredients, but by the fact that most manufacturers now put their food in cans with ring pulls.

Try to collect as many pans as you can and make sure they are good quality ones. The secret to keeping pans in good condition is to never overheat them. Start on a low heat and never have a flame going up the side of the pan. Also never plunge a hot pan into cold water and always clean them properly. Washing soda will remove most stains without having to scrub away at the metal.

Knives are really the most important tools you can get in the kitchen. Make sure you have a good set of very sharp knives and that you know how to sharpen them. You need a good stone for making the edge itself and a steel for keeping that edge. You keep a knife sharp by running along the steel at an angle of 20° to the steel with a very light pressure. Repeat for both sides of the knife with about a dozen strokes per side. All you are doing is realigning the microscopic bevels of the blade.

If the blade is blunt you need to draw it across a lubricated stone. Around 20 strokes on either side at 20° will create an edge.

Notes on the Resources

This book is not about bashing the supermarkets. What it is about is empowerment. Many of the ingredients refered to can be bought comfortably at supermarkets, especially items like washing soda and bicarbonate of soda etc. These are probably going to be your first point of call anyway. Some products are nearly all basic chemicals anyway. Strong bleach is often 11% Sodium Hypochlorite. If you dilute this twenty times you will have a perfectly good sterilising liquid, but make sure you are well protected from splashes to clothes, eyes and skin in the process! Shop clever and look at the ingredients. You will soon be making up your own recipes for all kinds of household materials.

However, it is not always possible to buy everything at the supermarket. In these cases you will get some hints and tips below. I have restricted my searches to the United States and the UK, but later editions might include other countries too. You can also go to www. precycle-it.co.uk where you will find continually updated information on recipes, materials and resources.

Sodium hypochlorite can be purchased as strong bleach, as described above, but it is much safer to make your own as in the chapter on household cleaners.

Bicarb, sodium bicarbonate or baking powder is widely available and can be bought in bulk from health stores. Borax or sodium borate is widely available in supermarkets and is also available in hardware shops and frequently on Ebay. In the UK try Wilkinsons Stores www.

Precycle!

wilkinsonplus.com (0845 6080807) and in the US try Ace Hardware on 1-866-5334 or at www.acehardware. com. If you have a good local market seek out the haba-dashers. These are often a forgotten Aladdin's Cave and are certainly well worth a visit.

Lye, or sodium hydroxide, is often sold as drain cleaner. It should be labelled as 99% sodium hydroxide. Any other ingredients apart from a little chalk for settling makes it unsuitable for soap making. This is available in most supermarkets and Wilkinsons in the UK or Ace Hardware again in the US. You can also try www.soapkitchenonline.co.uk. in the UK and www.snowdriftfarm.com (toll free on 888-999-6950) in the US.

Both of these companies are good for general glycerine soap resources too and liquid glycerine is widely available from pharmacies and herb shops, but not so much in supermarkets.

All manner of essential oils are readily available from health shops or cosmetic companies. Make sure that the oil comes from a reputable supplier, but bear in mind that the cheaper ones will often have other oils added to them, thus diluting both their fragrance and their effectiveness. Do not buy any essential oil unless the bottle points out that the contents are "Pure Essential Oil."

Lanolin is described in the book as being something you can make by washing a sheepskin. Sheepskins are available from people who keep sheep, obviously, and you can find these online. Try various spinning sites and organisations for sheepskins and yarns and you will have more than you need. These days it costs more money to shear a sheep than the coat is actually worth, so there are plenty of people out there looking to sell. You can buy lanolin itself from various outlets. In the UK try www. head2toez.co.uk (tel: 0700 3451517) or www.herbspro.

com (1-866-915-5300) in the US.

For more information on herbs, growing herbs and using them in food and cosmetics have a look at the Herb Society of London at www.herbsociety.co.uk where you will find lots of hints and tips as well as the opportunity to join one of the world's great bodies.

Aloes are plants that grow all over the world, especially in arid regions. They are wonderful for all skin problems and rejuvenating the skin. They are particularly good on burns (though in the book we give guidelines to be sure a burn gets appropriate medical treatment). You can buy aloe plants from garden centres and they make great house plants. When they have grown you can use the juice in the leaves yourself. Simply slice a piece off and squeeze it; the juice will come out. All pharmacies also stock aloe vera gel which is perfect for use in our recipes. They also sell aloe vera drink for people with tummy problems, which is an extremely good treatment.

Epsom salts can be obtained from pharmacies as they are used as a laxative.

Jam making equipment is useful for making sauces and other cooking too. Maslin pans (large, heavy bottomed pans with a wide open gape), jam thermometers, jelly bags and muslin sheets are all widely available, especially from good cooking shops. Online try Crocks and Pots in the UK at www.crocksandpots.co.uk (0208 1445517) or in the US try Homestead Harvest at www.homestead-harvest.com (1-877-300-3427).

Sausage making equipment and curing salt is more popular and more widely available than ever before. In the UK and US there are a number of companies specialising not only on the mail order provision of materials but also selling specialised spices that you can use to

Precycle!

make anything from a wet sausage to beef jerky with little fuss and complete certainty of its safety. In the UK try Weschenfelder at www.weschenfelder.co.uk (tel: 01642 247524) and in the US try The Sausage Maker Inc. at www.sausagemaker.com (888-490-8525).

Mushroom growing spores and kits are available from The Rustic Mushroom Company rustic_mushrooms@btinternet.com (01435 860935)

Local honey is full of local minerals and pollen which offers great health benefits, particularly for people suffering from asthma. Supermarket honey often comes from China, Russia or Australia. For local honey look in the library or check your search engine for your nearest beekeeping association. They often rely on honey sales to keep afloat, so you will be welcomed. These organisations are also the best places to buy beeswax and, who knows, you might just get interested in beekeeping too!

Pig's trotters are really difficult to find now as they have gone out of fashion and people no longer have the knowledge, or the interest, in using them. They are needed mostly to make great pie jelly. In the UK, and similarly in the US, butchers have gone out of business in great numbers and so, if you find a butcher, order your trotters well in advance.

Rennet is widely available in the UK from Ascot Smallholding Supplies at www.ascott.biz (0845 1306285) or Smallholder Supplies at www.smallholdersupplies.co.uk (01476 870070). In the US try The Cheese Supply Company at www.cheesesupply.com. You do not have to use animal rennet now since all kinds of different rennets are available, some vegetarian in origin. Both of these companies are good for the supply of cheese making equipment and presses that can be used for fruit pressing too.